**Karen C.**

*5 out of 5 stars* ★★★★★

*Incredible Journey*

It is amazing how our world makes us believe life should be one way, but all the while we know it should be different. Kristin and Peter share their journey of reordering their lives and the peace and joy which comes when the world as we know it slips away. Exceptional story of their incredible faith and the love of God that truly wants what is best for us (no matter how painful that might be at the time) and wants us to enjoy the gift of the life we are given. Wonderful, thought provoking, and inspiring adventure!

**Taylor S.**

*5 out of 5 stars* ★★★★★

*The best book I've read in years!*

Highly recommend this book!! So inspiring and enlightening! Kristin and Peter's journey is so beautifully told and I can't wait to read about more of their adventures in the future!

**Leigh R.**

*5 out of 5 stars* ★★★★★

*Journey of a lifetime*

Well written book with thought provoking insights. The reader can visualize the sights, hear the sounds, taste the food, and enjoy the journey with the author. Well done.

**S. Morris**

*5 out of 5 stars* ★★★★★

**A joy to read!**

Inspiring and introspective! Kristin and Peter's Camino became my Camino! Sharing wonderful interpersonal truths and sparking my curiosity! Well done.


**Kay H.**

*5 out of 5 stars* ★★★★★

**Well worth the money**

I have enjoyed this book so much. I loved having Kristin on our morning news in Tulsa. This book is a must read. I didn't want to put it down. Well worth the money.


**Sheena G.**

*5 out of 5 stars* ★★★★★

**A spiritual adventure**

I was very surprised at the ending of the book. We went from struggling to triumph. What an interesting read.


**Anna B.**

*5 out of 5 stars* ★★★★★

**Heartwarming!**

I enjoyed reading this book. The author was authentic and shared her experiences in a way that was enjoyable to read and thought provoking.

# My Journey Back To God

## Written While on Pilgrimage Across the Camino de Santiago, Israel and India

Cyndi + Nick,

Enjoy the journey!

Kristin Dickerson

Edited by Kristen Roybal

Cover design and illustration by Matthew McCollom

Contact information:

Website: SpiritAndNatureProductions.com

YouTube: Spirit and Nature Productions with Kristin & Peter

Instagram: KristinDickersonTV

Facebook: Kristin Dickerson TV

This book is dedicated to Paramahansa Yogananda.

Thank you for helping me find my way back to God.

# Contents

# Preface

As we neared the final 100 miles of the Camino de Santiago, the call to journal was made very clear. So, I started writing, and my testimony flowed out of me.

As I transcribed this hand-written journal after I got back to the US, I noticed a consistency in what came to me during our three-month pilgrimage across Spain, Israel and India. At first, my mind would often focus on a challenge (past or present), then as I wrote, the lesson would come. Some lessons stem from choices in my past, which are not all flattering, but as the Bob Dylan lyrics that kept coming to me on the Camino declared, "you've got no secrets to conceal."

My husband, Peter, and I both grew up with the teachings of Jesus Christ. As adults, we've been learning about the commonalities between Christianity, Hinduism and Buddhism, which we got to experience first hand on this pilgrimage. In this journal, we'll make reference to Paramahansa Yogananda. He is an Indian guru who is credited with bringing Kriya yoga to the US. His meditation techniques and "how to live" lessons helped me find my way back to God and continue to guide my life.

When we embarked on this pilgrimage, our goal was to dedicate time to experiencing God in various forms. We didn't know how He would reveal Himself—we just hoped that He would.

# Spain

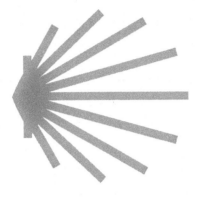

# "Y te Llama"

## *Day 29*

## *Ponferrada, León, Spain*

We're sitting outside a church. Above the door it says, "El Maestro está aquí, y te llama." The teacher is here, and he calls you.

Thoughts come about the power of a whisper. Shouting, "I love you," compared to a whisper, "I love you."

Yesterday, we briefly met a woman from Louisville, Kentucky on a mountain decline. It was a hard stretch. After a brief introduction, she gave us a business card. On one side it had a picture of a pine tree growing from the side of a rocky mountain. The other side of the card had these words, "'You can't!' shouted the rock. 'Just watch me' whispered the tree.'"

There's so much power in restraint. Control.

I had a dream about my former boss. He came to the office to ask forgiveness. Later, a crowd of women said they wouldn't hear him. I pleaded with the crowd to allow an opportunity for understanding and they obliged, but he didn't follow through.

# Getting Started

## *Day 30*

## *Cacabelos, León, Spain*

In the last 24-ish hours I've heard, "Are you journaling?" at least three times. My answer was basically, "no," so I took that as a hint from Divine Mother. I mentally told God I needed paper and immediately realized I'd been carrying it the whole time—in the form of 24 talent-release pages in my backpack.

As we meditated outside a church while listening to a Krishna Das song in our headphones, thoughts came. I wrote them on a talent release page, which was my first entry in this journal.

Immediately after meditating and journaling, we were given a Divine gift in the form of a pastelería. We saw the amazing baked treats in the window. Realizing it was close to siesta (two minutes away from the store closing for an afternoon break), I pushed the door and it appeared locked. Moments later, a customer walked past me, pushed the door and it opened right away. We followed the customer inside, ordered pastries filled with homemade creams and covered in sugar of various forms, then ate them while sitting on a bench, underneath a tree near the store. The desserts were the best yet. What a gift—and right after I moved forward on journaling.

Today was the best day yet. We went the farthest, walked the slowest, possibly laughed the most, and really took in the environments around us. We bought a ticket to tour a castle, had second and third breakfasts, drank double café con leches (and ate the lemon cakes that accompanied them), had more conversations during the day and truly savored our Camino.

# The Last 100 Miles

## Day 30

## Cacabelos, León, Spain

Now 75% complete, 118 miles left. As soon as I learned we had 130-ish miles left to walk, my perspective completely changed. The end was coming. All of a sudden, the Camino was not this never-ending repetitive walk. It was something to be cherished because it was almost over. I need to do that with life—live life like it's almost over—not that it's never ending.

Leaving my job as a news reporter and anchor at NBC-5 in Dallas-Fort Worth was so much fun. Not just because of the free pizza and double potlucks with my weekend co-workers. But I truly savored the experience because I knew it was ending.

My co-workers reacted differently as well. It seemed like people were more open to connect, share, spend time together; long-planned dinners and chai dates were finally accomplished. I'd wished that those relationships were prioritized earlier.

There's freedom knowing something is coming to an end because you can give it your all. You won't run out of energy or get overwhelmed. Like knowing it's the last few strides of a run—or for me—my senior year of college competing as an equestrian.

Going into the Camino, I said I wanted to make time to connect with people. At times I've also felt very quiet and

5

wanted to hide within myself. But I've also learned—especially at meal times—conversations are so much better with more people; the more varied the better. "Come join us! You alone?" is usually how it might start. Soon after, we're learning about the landscape and society issues of a far-off country, while laughing at what we have in common as pilgrims and as humans—most often it's an appreciation for food, coffee and getting to sit down.

Challenge: how do I live life like I'm ending it (ending the Camino, ending a job)?

Will facing death feel this way? Knowing I'm going to miss the sweet faces of friends, but excited for what's next to come on my journey.

# Pain

## *Day 30*
## *Cacabelos, León, Spain*

Pain has sparked an appreciation for health. I normally don't think about my ability to walk with ease (with exception to having to wear mandatory beige high heels on the news-anchor desk). A little pain reminds me of the miracle of the body. The knees, ankles, feet, joints, and tendons all working together to move me forward to the next spot—or even having to double back if the brain forgot something. Same theme—appreciation for something because you know you're at risk of losing it.

I have so many bug bites. So very many.

# Processing

## *Day 30*
## *Cacabelos, León, Spain*

Why the Camino is helpful for emotional processing: one tiny thing happens, one stranger says one sentence that strikes you, your brain reminds you of something from your past, and then you spend the next five kilometers staring at the ground (often in challenging footing) or staring at the mountains or the Meseta thinking about that one thing. So, nothing is buried or stored to process later. Things come up, they percolate, which is then heated in the fire of physical exhaustion and sweat equity—and those things are cooked, processed and set aside for good. It's really helpful. And the processing doesn't stop once you reach your albergue (group living-quarters for pilgrims) or hotel for the night. Because that's when you chat with even more people who might say something that sparks a new topic to process, or, like what happens to me, issues come up and are resolved in my dreams.

# Booze

## *Day 30*

## *Cacabelos, León, Spain*

I haven't drank alcohol in almost four years. I was, what I've now learned to accept as a label, an alcoholic from 13 to 33 years old. My interpretation of my alcoholism was I would rarely have one drink without craving many more. Example: one beer would lead to shots of alcohol, then either making myself puke or do drugs so I could drink more.

I don't remember ever really thinking I was addicted to drinking until I realized how difficult it was to not drink. After quitting, I craved wine and beer for a solid year and a half. Daily for the first year. It got easier around six months of sobriety. The easiest day was the day after my last drink because I was so incredibly sick. The night before, I had almost lost everything—career, relationships.

While preparing for the Camino, we heard a lot about the local wine and how it could sometimes be cheaper than a bottle of water.

There's also something especially delicious about a cold beer after a long day of walking in the heat. That first beer was always so good, and it made the many that would follow easier to drink. I pondered—can I drink during the Camino? I literally considered that for some time. But, I gave up booze as an offering to God. Now, I am walking the Camino in an effort to find and get closer to Him—so the two did not "pair well," as they say in wine terms. No boozing on the Camino—or likely, ever again.

I was missing alcohol while walking the first 20-plus days. I thought, "Why did I have to give it up?" It looked and smelled so enticing, and everyone else appeared to be drinking. Then Peter and I were unexpectedly invited to join a couple from California, Jen and Randy, for dinner. We had met them for the first time just an hour before.

Jen is 30-ish years sober, a member and mentor in Alcoholics Anonymous. Neither of us ordered wine at dinner. She said alcohol helped her reach rock bottom. She lost everything: her home, her marriage—all of it. She described her drinking tendencies and they sounded the same as mine—she couldn't have just one.

She said, "You just need to change your perspective. It isn't 'I can't or don't GET to drink anymore,' it should be "I don't HAVE TO drink anymore.'" Truth.

Alcohol was a helper—socially, anxiety, stress relief, courage. It was a booster shot for celebration or loss; however, for me, it was a wild card.

One morning in my teens, I remember waking up and calling my best friend to ask, "Did we have fun last night?" On a rougher morning in my 20s, I called a police-officer friend and asked him to check any police reports because I vaguely remembered crying in an ambulance. There was one report for a girl at my apartment building, but the age was listed as 14 and not 24. Apparently, she was lost and was banging on a neighbor's apartment door trying to get in. Poor 14 year old—or drunk 24 year old. I still have a scar on my ankle from whatever happened that night.

I was living without purpose, wasting time with distractions. Why was I risking my life?

It wasn't until I started practicing Bikram yoga that everything started to shift. Bikram yoga is a hot yoga class that includes the same 26 postures and breathing exercises in a 105-degree room. It's hard.

Bikram yoga forced my brain to focus and my body to feel like it was struggling to survive—those two things combined, somehow allowed my mind to quiet and my soul to start speaking up.

Extreme moments of clarity still come during yoga classes—not all, but most. Those moments provide answers to problems, empathy for people I'm frustrated with, separation from anything I'm attached to, and often a broader perspective on any life situation I'm in. For me, it's similar to therapy with psychedelic mushrooms, which I'll get to later.

After starting Bikram yoga, I started thinking "There's gotta be something more to life." I also found meditation, married Peter, quit drinking, got several job promotions, got hired in Dallas, and now I'm continuing a quest for a more consistent inner peace.

Again, "I don't have to drink anymore."

# How We Got Here

## Day 32

### Pradela, León, Spain

For the 15 months before walking the Camino de Santiago, Peter and I were actively looking for signs. We had just spent three weeks in India for meditation and counseling with a friend who is a monk. Things at work had become unpredictable and I was starting to wonder what life would be like outside of TV-news.

One day my boss was in a horrible mood. I stood up to him in a meeting and asked him what he wanted from us because he was so unhappy.

He then called me into his office and for 20-ish minutes pointed out that I'd never be good enough.

The thing that hurt the most was that he implied I hadn't worked hard. For the last 15 years before that moment, that's all I did was work hard.

I prided myself on volunteering to work nearly every holiday, filling in for anyone who called in sick, shooting stories on my own time, including while on vacation across the country, or out of the country. I'd given everything I had to my craft, and despite the numerous national awards and an employee of the month honor, which he nominated me for, all of a sudden, I would never be good enough.

Toward the end of that 20-minute verbal beat down, a few tears trickled down my cheek. It took everything I had just to say, "So, I'll never be good enough? Is there anything else?"

I walked out of his office, went to my desk that was two cubicles away from his and sat down.

Moments later, he slowly walked behind me. I could feel that he was standing up straighter, his chest larger. He felt great. I, however, had been gutted.

Everything I knew to be true—including my identity as an award-winning journalist, TV anchor, reporter and photographer—was now in question.

I walked to my car and had (what felt like) a panic attack. Once my breathing came back under control, I walked back inside to anchor the 5 o'clock news for someone on vacation.

Days later, we left for India. The trip changed from a relaxing meditation retreat, to deep soul-searching and life council.

We had previously learned a prayer in India for people who, in this case, bother you. The prayer is done five times a day: when waking up, eating breakfast, lunch, dinner, and before going to sleep. To perform this prayer, you basically imagine the person surrounded with light for a solid minute and silently chant "om, peace, harmony." So, I had to do this for my boss. I prayed so hard for that SOB. Every day, five times a day, for three weeks he had my complete focus and (attempted) goodwill.

After I returned from India, he had changed his tune. He told me he was proud of me for winning another National Gracie Award, and confided that he was having some challenges outside of work. But I was already mentally prepared for a life transition.

Peter and I went to New York City to accept a Gracie award for a story I had reported, shot, and edited.

During that trip, the word "roam" kept coming to us. In our hotel, all of the miniature soaps and shampoos said, "roam." During the awards ceremony, the word was mentioned, and someone named Roam or Rome was honored. Then on our flight home, we sat next to a woman who was on her way home from Rome. Over and over, we heard it or saw it: roam.

We soon drove to Tulsa for a weekend and talked it over with our dear friend Yvonne Lewis. She is a former news anchor, a preacher, and licensed professional counselor with a master's degree in Divinity. The title I would give her is Master in detecting the presence of the Holy Spirit. She's written a book about her faith walk called *31 Stories that Build Faith*. On its pages, she talks about feeling "God bumps," and how the Holy Spirit and God have guided her life. Reading it, changed my perception of God in an incredible way by making it much easier to see His hand at work in my life.

We sat in Yvonne's living room and told her about the conversation in my boss's office, India, and finally—the signs of "roam." She said she felt the Holy Spirit sweep into the room. I already had chills before she put words to the physical manifestation of the Holy Spirit's presence. She confirmed what we were thinking, and we needed to get ready to roam. That means we would need to prepare for a move. She said to be like a butterfly and get light, So, we got mobile.

We sold our house, downsized our belongings and moved into a tiny apartment around the corner from work.

The morning that we signed the paperwork to sell our house, a mandatory afternoon meeting was called at work. Our general manager announced that my boss had been fired. No reason was given.

We first heard about the Camino de Santiago from Peter's grandmother, whom we lovingly call Nana. She's a special woman. When you walk into her presence she yells, "darlin'!" opens her arms and awaits an embrace. She has bright red hair, sings Frank Sinatra without invitation, and is to credit for Peter's extreme sweetness, because she helped raise him alongside Peter's mom, Ilona. Nana is also incredibly spiritual and open minded.

She gave Peter a book written by Shirley MacLaine (Academy Award winning actress and best-selling author). The book, *The Camino: A Journey of the Spirit*, was Shirley's account of her experience walking the Camino in 1994.

Throughout this faith walk, which had me quitting my career in TV-news, I found that God always put the absolute best person into our path to help guide or encourage us.

That included encouragement from Shirley MacLaine. One news connection led to another, and I was given a phone number that could lead to Shirley MacLaine. I called, and she answered. It took a minute to convince her to talk to me, and for her to admit it was actually her. But her voice is unmistakable. I can't tell you how many times I've heard it while watching her 1989 movie *Steel Magnolias* on television growing up.

Each time she answered my call, she told me what she was doing. The first time she said she was in the middle of an eye exam, the next time she mentioned she was having lunch with friends—both times she asked me to call back so we could speak, which we finally did.

She gave us advice on how to survive the Camino, including, "take care of your feet and wear a really big hat!" What an incredible lady.

Everything about our Camino preparation was like we were going to open a window and a barn door would fly open. For instance, I was randomly asked to be a first-time guest faculty member at a weekend training for the National Press Photographers Association. There I was, in a room with the best storytellers and news photographers in the country who were more than happy to help me plan how to shoot a three-month pilgrimage. They also suggested that our video should focus on me and Peter, not solely on the experiences of other pilgrims.

One more example: we stopped by a camera store to look for a small light to take with us on the pilgrimage. When we walked in, an expert in lighting and still photography was visiting from the east coast and was in town teaching a class on lighting in all conditions.

We watched the class, then he connected with us afterward, asked about our pilgrimage plan, showed us the holes in it and how to better prepare. We also walked out of there with a whole new set of upgraded camera gear.

So, when it was clear (over and over) that we needed to prepare to roam, we also started to be shown that we should be prepared to shoot video and record sound of the experiences that lie ahead.

# Laura

## Day 35

## Triacastela, Galicia, Spain

Peter is having some pain in his shins, so we booked him a massage. We walked half a day, which was in the rain, so it counts as double in my opinion.

I'm sitting outside at a restaurant in Triacastela. The tables are on the side of a narrow street that isn't wide enough for cars, just people walking. My tea just arrived. It's black tea that came in a boxed sachet with steamed milk in a separate silver pot. The tea glass is double-walled, so it doesn't sweat. It reminds me of the set of glasses Peter owned when I met him. They were part of the bulk disposal that happened when we downsized in preparation for the unknown adventure that was ahead. We didn't know exactly what we were preparing for, we just knew we needed to get rid of any extra weight.

My cheese just arrived. It's enough to be shared by several people. Queso de O Cebreiro is the dish's name. O Cebreiro is a town we recently walked through (the first part by horse, which garnered one stink-eye by a sassy pilgrim climbing the same path). The man who owns the horses, said the cheese is the town's specialty.

It's smooth, creamy and served with either honey or a red marmalade made of quince fruit. It's making my mouth water just writing about it.

The sun was just out for a moment, but I can still see the dark clouds above the mountains that brought challenges to our morning walk. Kind of like knowing I'm in a good place now, but there are dark things from my past that can still cloud my mind.

Dark—as in sadness. The only word I could find to describe it to people was "darkness." Sometimes I didn't even realize it was there until months after it was gone.

I can feel it coming on. The temper shortens, my face flattens (as compared to being round during a smile). Peter says he can see it happening and calls it, "putting up my wall."

If God is warmth, openness, trust and love—this is the opposite of that. I don't enjoy it; however, some part of my being must love it—maybe the part that hates everything, everyone, and doesn't want to be here anymore. That's the worst part—the thought that I don't want to be here anymore.

The darkness has this similarity to drinking: if it gets past the early stages, it stays a while and it's even harder to get out of it.

It just started raining.

The key is catching it quickly.

In the first few days of our Camino, and the days prior to starting, there were challenges. Relatively small challenges, but big enough to test my inner peace and calm. The peace that finally arrived and is now maintained through Kriya yoga meditation and extreme physical exertion through Bikram yoga.

One test that came early was a salty airline employee who appeared to be ruining many travelers' days by charging them an unexpected $100 to check their backpacks instead of carrying them on the airplane. She almost got my peace when she got my $100.

The second night of our Camino, we arrived in Roncesvalles exhausted.

I carelessly set my mini-tourist purse that held my passport and $1,000 on a ledge by my bed.

The next morning, I woke up late. I hadn't properly packed the night before, so I rushed out of the albergue half-awake and half-aware. That night, we checked into an albergue and they didn't ask to see my passport, which is rare.

A day later, I realized I hadn't seen my passport in a while. I looked through my backpack, Peter looked through his. I was already planning the steps of how to get a new passport—realizing how it was going to derail our trip for the next week, minimum.

I got so mad at myself. Then I found it.

My little grey passport-purse had wedged itself in-between two sections of my backpack and it was as safe as a bug in a rug. But my mind was already starting to go into that dark space.

We tried to re-group. Peter and I started walking quietly (both still frustrated with the "what if" we'd just experienced) when we heard a beautifully loud and cheerful voice with a British accent yell from a balcony above us, "goooooood mooooooorning!"

There's no way to not smile when a bouquet of joyful energy is unexpectedly thrown at you from above. It was Laura. Her infectious happiness helped snap me out of my state of darkness.

19

The first time we met Laura, we were halfway up a mountain on the first day of our Camino—struggling to hike from Saint-Jean-Pied-de-Port to Orisson, France. We'd already eaten all of the food we carried for that day. Peter and I saw a lone apple tree and collected a few of its fruit that were beneath it on the ground. We chose a spot to sit down together in the shade on the opposite side of the road.

Not long after we sat down, Laura joined us. At that point, I doubt we were the ones to invite her, but we were grateful for her company. This was the first time I learned to accept anything she offered us, because I'd need those offerings in the future (food, medical supplies, etc.). Laura just seemed to know what we needed to make us better.

The most significant time we crossed paths with Laura was in the small village of Zabaldika. It's home to a 1300s historic church, which is supported by a group of sweet nuns from the Society of the Sacred Heart. Their church and albergue is just off the current Camino trail; however, they pointed out that historically, the trail would bring pilgrims right next to their door.

As we climbed the steps up to the church (panting), we were greeted by that beautifully loud British voice that accompanies her blonde curly hair and sunburned skin. I'm not sure of Laura's age, but she has a daughter a bit younger than me, and also a young granddaughter who she cherishes.

That night inside the church, the pilgrims all sat together in a circle and the nuns guided us through a prayer and spiritual reading in several languages. We were all invited to share something about our Camino or why we were walking. The most touching moment came from a man from South Africa who talked about losing his wife and struggling to get past that loss. It sounded like he hoped the Camino would help him move forward.

I felt like I had absolutely nothing to share and was confident that the sister would not call on me as long as I didn't make eye contact at key moments. I was wrong.

She called on me. Laura was sitting on the bench behind me and I heard her giggle. I looked at her and she waved her pointer finger at me admitting she'd silently suggested to the nun that I get called on. Again, Laura always seems to know what I need before I need it.

Immediately, I had something to say. I also knew I needed to say it as slowly and simply as possible because it would be translated for some of the others including the sisters.

I said this: "I have a tendency to get depressed or sad. On the Camino, when I would start to get depressed, I'd see Laura. She would cheer for me and snap me out of it. I need to learn how to be Laura for myself. I need to be the one who cheers for me and lifts me up. I need to be more like Laura."

That night in the church's albergue, I dreamed I was killed in a car wreck. I wasn't paying attention to the road and the vehicle went sideways quickly. I knew it wasn't good because I was going so fast. I was then pushed into a building, but there wasn't a crash; it was like I was going through a blurred-grey tunnel that kept speeding up.

In the next scene of the dream, I was in a waiting room. It looked like a 1980s-style business office. It was a large, circular room with chairs around the outer wall. I was alone.

I realized I was dead, and I figured that was a good thing because I might get to meet God or our Guru, Paramahansa Yogananda. So, I waited.

Guruji came in, but his brown skin was light like it was painted. He looked different, but I knew it was him.

I also knew my body was being worked on somewhere else. Every now and then, I'd feel weakness in my arm or a part of the body. I knew

people were trying to help my body, but it wasn't happening where I was.

My next memory was similar to the third *Matrix* movie when Keanu Reeves' character, Neo, brings Trinity back to life. In my case, two giant hands entered a digital version of my body and pumped my heart—bringing me back to life.

When I woke up, the albergue was blaring one of Bob Dylan's greatest hits, "The Times They Are A-Changin'."

My brain was finally fully-awake when I walked down the steps to breakfast. I found myself singing along to, "How does it feel? To be on your own, with no direction home, like a complete unknown."

That Dylan song continued to come to me at various times throughout my Camino, including at the very end as we walked through Santiago. It was the weirdest thing.

I told Peter and Laura about my dream, about the large hands grasping my heart and bringing me back to life after the car wreck. Peter said, "It's like you were resurrected."

If so, I hope the long-residing darkness within my mind died that night in Zabaldika.

My hope is that those hands brought me back to life without that part of me—allowing the truer version of me to reside and continue seeking God, His presence, His peace, His guidance. Because when that darkness is ruling over my mind, the only thing that is allowed in is more darkness—in the form of anger, jealousy, self-doubt and depression.

I need to confirm this to myself: a part of me died that night in Zabaldika. That part of me died that night in Zabaldika.

# My Meseta

## *Day 35*

## *Triacastela, Galicia, Spain*

I'm writing this journal entry 27 days after that dream and I haven't experienced the darkness again, but it came close on the Meseta.

That long stretch of terrain can be a brain buster for some— for others, it's the most enjoyable part of their trip. For me, it was a challenge.

When we started the Camino, it felt like I was in a photographer's theme park where all the rides were free and there weren't any lines. I was also tall enough to ride. There were new sights, sounds, and smells every mile or so as we traversed through the mountains that were home to countless farm animals wearing various bells that sounded like a heavenly symphony.

Then there was the Meseta. It was warmer, drier, home to few animals, and the landscape (in my opinion) got a bit boring, which made it more challenging for me to find its beauty. Since I didn't have the distraction of a camera lens, my mind matched the physical challenges of walking, with memories of past situations that were also challenging.

I thought of Peter's dad. A few years ago, he came to live with us for one month, but he stayed for 18 months. Kicking him out, meant Peter would have to stand up to the father who had left his family when Peter was little. It also meant Peter would have to pick his wife over his father.

There was a period of time—maybe 13 months—when I didn't know what Peter's choice would be. That was hard. That was very hard.

During one stretch of the Meseta, I thought about the difficulty of that time. I thought about how his father almost ended our marriage. How could I have almost let that happen? That's when I broke. I tossed my walking sticks down, unsnapped and off-loaded my backpack onto the side of the trail and wept.

As I held my eyes with the palms of my hands, fingertips to my forehead, elbows on my knees and butt in the dirt, I cried.

What really frustrated me was my inability to speak up for myself during the time he lived with us. Why couldn't I just say, "Get out of my house! Why don't you pay rent? Get off my couch. Get a job. Volunteer. Stop spending money on my credit card. Apologize to Peter's mom." I could've said any of those things to him, but I didn't.

One day, I was venting to my hairdresser and she asked me why I couldn't just say something? It was a perfect question.

For some reason, after I quit drinking and ejecting deep-rooted frustrations while intoxicated, that energy materialized in my throat. So when I was sober and angry, it would feel like my throat was closing, my jaw tightening. I literally couldn't get a word out.

The one time his dad and I got into an argument, I raised my voice at him for not watching our dog while she was in the yard and she ate a bunch of flowers. It's such a trivial thing. When he yelled back, I froze like a fainting goat.

Since I have no plans to give Peter's dad equal space here to plead his case and share stories about what it was like living with me—I'll move on.

After I broke down and cried on the trail, I got really sick that night. Vomiting started around midnight and continued into the morning.

Pilgrims were supposed to leave that albergue by 8 a.m. I thought I could walk the Camino, but then the diarrhea started at 7:50 a.m. Nope. I wasn't leaving.

I finally made it to the main-floor lobby. Peter found me a small trash can to keep near me while he tried to explain I was sick and needed to stay, but there was a language barrier. The volunteer spoke Italian, which didn't help our English nor our weak Spanish.

When the volunteer arrived in the lobby with us, a wave of nausea came over me and the final remains of the previous night's dinner went spewing into the tiny trash can. No translation needed.

Thankfully, the albergue's volunteers were very accommodating.

Is the mental and emotional processing that happened on the trail, tied to my body purging itself hours later? I'm choosing to believe the two are related (especially because Peter ate the same things I did for dinner). I'm hoping that, again, something within me died or was officially left behind on the Camino. This time it was in the town of Astorga.

# Sesame

## Day 37

## Portomarín, Galicia, Spain

Two months after we received the message to "roam," we were moving forward on trying to figure out how to do it. We sold our house, which forced Peter's dad to move out and into a college friend's house on the other side of the country. We had a garage sale that helped us get rid of a chunk of our belongings so we could transition from a 2,200-square-foot house to a roughly 900-square-foot apartment.

We were getting ready to launch and were just waiting for the signal to fly. Then I missed a period. What in the world? Peter and I had been trying to conceive for roughly four years. We'd get the courage, feel stable and enthused to become parents, but then it just wouldn't happen. So, we gave up.

We weren't quite ready to take a step in the medical direction for help; Peter had also mentioned several times that we could just adopt a teenager one day who really needed parents (even if the adoption was more in the form of friendship and advice and not in the form of paperwork and legal counsel).

So, we were stunned but grateful for the unexpected change and need for stability, which doesn't involve flying in any sense of the word. We're a bit earthy-crunchy, so after three pregnancy tests gave us a "+," we went to see our iridologist (who looks at my eyeballs and tells me what nutrients I need).

Years before, she looked into my eyes for the first time. She asked me about a small fracture in my tailbone—a detail about my childhood no one would know about. The fracture was caused when I fell off a horse and landed on my tailbone, hitting the hard ground after riding near my grandfather's ranch in Lordsburg, New Mexico.

When she asked about that private piece of medical history— I was sold, and she's helped guide my nutritional needs for years. This time when I saw her, and before I could share any personal news, she said, "Oh I had a feeling something was changing. You're about seven weeks along."

An unexpected trip home to New Mexico had me sitting in my mom's car going through a bank drive-thru so she could make a deposit. As we waited for the teller to check her paperwork, I unintentionally told my mom that I had quit drinking coffee for 40 days and on day 30-something, I got pregnant. She said, "you're pregnant?" and continued to have the most beautiful and loving emotional breakdown that I'd bet that bank teller had ever seen or heard in her drive-thru.

My favorite part of my mom's reaction was when she realized the baby might have dimples like me, and her, and her mother. I'm not sure at what point I joined her in the tears, but they were flowing, and it was wonderful.

That enthusiasm also greeted us at our obstetrician's office. There was a mix-up in booking my appointment and the nurse thought I was just there for a routine checkup. When we explained that we thought we were pregnant she tested my urine sample, came back into the room and cheered, "You did it! Great job, you two!"

We nicknamed the baby Sesame, because that was its size and Peter lovingly started referencing it as that—Sesame.

The nurse asked if we wanted to try and see the baby even though the appointment wasn't booked for that. The doctor just happened to be free, which she explained was extremely rare, and he was more than happy to do an ultrasound for us.

He pointed out what he saw on a screen, which looked like it was on a computer from the late 90s.

Looking inside me, he pointed out there was a sack, which he measured and confirmed was about 7-8 weeks along. But he kept talking. His tone softened. His sentences got longer. He just kept talking.

I wondered, why isn't Peter taking a picture of the screen? I nudged him to do so and he silently motioned to me to wait or slow down.

Oh. Why? Is something wrong? Something is wrong. When the doctor left the room, Peter and I stared at each other, cried for a moment and hugged.

It's called a blighted ovum. My body was preparing for a pregnancy, but there was no embryo. There's no living baby.

Our friend, mentor and counselor, Yvonne, saw the printout from the ultrasound and she said it looked like an angel's wing. Before she said that, I had already had a version of a Paul McCartney song on repeat in my head. "Blackbird singing in the dead of night. Take these broken wings and learn to fly. Blackbird fly."

The decision to remove the miscarriage via surgery was made a few days before Christmas. I was working through the holidays and I wouldn't have an opportunity for the surgery until after I was done co-hosting a New Year's Eve special.

**Facebook Post:**

*What I learned from having a miscarriage:*

*In early November, my husband and I learned we were pregnant with our first child—a hope that had been underlying for the past four years. The end of December, we learned our pregnancy was likely going to end in a miscarriage . . . and on the 4th of January, it did.*

*A friend told me months ago about a type of therapy that has you revisit something traumatic in your life and you ask yourself, "where was Jesus in the room?" Just writing that question makes me cry, because in this case—He was everywhere.*

*On the morning I'm writing this, I received a D&C, which basically removes the failed pregnancy, at Texas Health Huguley Hospital. When I arrived, the top sheet of my check-in paperwork read, "A prayer before surgery." Soon after, a chaplain came to pray with us. All of the doctors, nurses and techs were as skilled at their jobs as they were kind and compassionate. After the surgery was over, a nurse gave me a hand-written note that said, "Kristin, I'm sorry for what you have been thru. I will be praying for you."*

*Jesus was also "in the room," working through countless people who love us: a dear friend who talked and texted me through what to expect based on her own experience, my family quickly transitioning from requests for a baby girl to extra unconditional love, and managers at work making sure I had time to recover both physically and emotionally.*

*I'll admit, one night after learning a miscarriage was inevitable, I silently yelled at God and asked, "Why did this have to happen?" Thankfully, those feelings of anger were replaced with peace by the next afternoon.*

*Although I don't have a clear answer to my question, "why?" I do know that I am so grateful. I'm grateful that I woke up after anesthesia. I'm grateful for the man in the waiting room holding my clothes in a plastic hospital bag and texting my family that the doctor said everything went well.*

*I'm grateful for medical care that detected I needed surgery before my body failed to work (and for the job that provides insurance to help me pay for it). I'm also grateful that, to me, this is a small struggle compared to what so many people have faced and are currently facing.*

*Finally, I'm grateful for perspective. I've gained immense empathy for mothers and families who have suffered loss in this way. If you are one of them, this experience (and a really kind nurse) taught me how to offer my support by simply saying, "I'm sorry for what you have been through, and I will be praying for you," and I will be.*

Years before, Yvonne said she saw herself in our lives until the birth of a baby. She had a vision of being in the delivery room and holding up the baby like in *The Lion King*. When I saw that a new version of *The Lion King* was coming out, I looked for the release date. It was scheduled to come out on the exact day of what would have been Sesame's due date. I cried.

When that day arrived, Peter had planned a celebration. We went on a date to see the movie and also opened a care package that Peter's mom sent us, which arrived the day before.

She didn't know the significance of that day, nor did she know that we had nicknamed the baby Sesame. We opened her package and there was only one thing inside—a giant bag of sesame chips.

God is so thoughtful.

# Psilocybin

## Day 37

## Portomarín, Galicia, Spain

Around the time of the pregnancy, Peter's college buddy took psychedelic mushrooms, had a wonderful time looking at nature and suggested Peter try it. Of all things, Peter is a researcher. So, he started looking into all-things mushrooms—specifically their healing properties. He ordered several books, listened to podcasts, followed fungi folks on social media—the whole thing.

He started sending me research articles from Johns Hopkins University. Their research basically proved that psilocybin mushrooms—when used with a specific dose, environment and mindset—could help improve cases of extreme depression (among other things). Many people who participated in their medical trials, also considered the treatment one of the most spiritual experiences of their lives.

On a whim, I sent an email to the Johns Hopkins team asking to do a story about their research on psilocybin mushrooms and its healing benefits. I knew when sending this email, that the likelihood of my boss actually approving the story idea, then paying to send me and a photographer across the country to Baltimore to shoot the story, which has absolutely no visuals because it's all in people's heads, and it is a Schedule 1 drug that is illegal in most states (as of this writing), the likelihood of getting a "yes" was nearly impossible. I was wrong.

The researchers at Johns Hopkins approved my interview request, my boss approved the story and the trip to Baltimore was scheduled for the end of January—a few days after I returned to work after medical leave for the miscarriage.

After being alcohol-free for three years, a choice to do illegal and mind-altering drugs was a decision I took very seriously. I'd had opportunities to take mushrooms when I was younger (I'm trying to remember if I'd actually been offered them, but I knew I could always find and purchase them if I had wanted). I just never felt mentally sound enough to be in such an altered state.

I certainly didn't want to have a so-called "bad trip" and be stuck in a torturous situation in my head for an extended period of time.

But I was now ready, and more than a decade of medical research proved that this experience could be beneficial.

On a totally separate note—I was afraid to do a story about the effects of something that I knew nothing about nor did I know what visuals to create. Or maybe I just told myself that—it's research! It's for the story! Either way, what a trip I was about to have.

I would fly out for the interview on a Wednesday or Thursday so I had the previous Monday to take the mushrooms. We bought them through social media and they arrived in the mail. Boy, times have changed since the last time I bought illegal drugs.

So why was I ready? I had a lot of questions for God; and if this proved, as the research suggested, to be one of the most spiritually significant experiences of my life, I hoped to talk to

Him. Why did we get pregnant if it wasn't meant to be? Why were we told to "roam" and then told to "stay" in the form of a pregnancy. What am I supposed to do with this life? So many questions.

After the miscarriage, for weeks, I often felt overwhelming love. There was also a moment a few days after the surgery when I found myself standing in the corner of a store crying with the darkest of thoughts in my mind, "I don't want to be here anymore."

But after I shared on Facebook what had happened and what I'd learned from the miscarriage—love and perspective flowed in abundance. I heard from so many women and men who had experienced loss. Several of their personal experiences were outright horrendous (some because of poor medical care).

The extra emotions can also be attributed to increased estrogen levels that we were told are common amongst blighted ovum cases.

So, all of these things contributed to me being full of love and gratitude, and open to what the experience might show me.

The psilocybin morning was spent relatively quiet and meditative. Peter set up our bedroom so we could follow Johns Hopkins researchers' process—laying down, eyes covered, calming music in my headphones, and someone sitting with me as a guide. Peter served that role and transcribed the experience. He also recorded audio of what I described to him, which proved helpful even though I can still visualize the entire experience. The beginning, maybe 45 minutes after taking two grams of psilocybin, was all about losing awareness of the body. Visually, it seemed like I was in a dark movie theater, but then the walls of the theater disappeared, and I was in an expansive space that was infinite.

I had waves of intense gratitude. I envisioned a recent news report of a teenager and an elder Native American man facing off during a protest in Washington, DC. When I saw that video on the news, it really bothered me. In my psychedelic vision, I saw what it could have been like if the two had put their tensions aside and joined together in prayer. How powerful that would have been. I wept thinking about that shared spiritual respect and how it could have positively influenced everyone who saw it.

I thought of the Dalai Lama. My drug-induced feelings of extreme empathy must be what he experiences all the time. How does he maintain that? It must be exhausting.

Then it was time. I was already shown a lot, but I was ready for my questions to be answered. I started with the biggest one and asked, "God, where are you?"

The same voice responded, "I'm right here."

I wept because I knew God had been with me the whole time. He was always right here—within me. He is in every ounce of my being. My Creator is who He created. He is in everything and everyone. God created man and man created music— God is music. God is everything.

I had a vision of the night Peter and I conceived. I walked to the bathroom and just above me was a sheer white energy that swept through me almost knocking or sweeping the pregnancy away, like with a broom. This message came, "Don't practice conceiving if you're not ready to receive life."

One more message also became clear, "God loves me and wants me to be happy." He doesn't care if I'm a news anchor. He just wants me to be happy.

The next day, I saw my (new) boss and told him I likely was not going to renew my contract. I'd be leaving that summer.

My psychedelic experience also changed how I see my body. At first, I realized I spend way too much time on it—I feed it too much, primp it too much.

My body is a silent partner and its only way of speaking up is through illness. So, I need to listen to its whispers. I slowly started to gain sympathy for the body. It's like a little puppy—I need to take care of it, and it'll do its best for me.

Finally, there was a thought about surgery. More than a decade ago, I thought my success as a TV personality would be improved if my body's measurements were more flattering. So, I had surgery. During my psychedelic trip, my body spoke up about one thing—it was about that. It basically said, "Why would you do that? You didn't even ask me." My body was so disappointed that my mind's opinion of my body, God's creation, was anything less than perfect. If God created me, why wouldn't my mind see my body as perfect, which is exactly how He made me?

From that day on, I stopped coloring my grey hair and longed for a time when makeup wasn't mandatory; because now, I really want to know, "What do I actually look like?" Underneath the years of cutting and coloring, tanning and bleaching—what does the person look like who God created? I want to see her, and at some point, I want to see her as beautiful.

**Facebook Post:**

*One of my superficial goals of walking the Camino was to figure out what I actually look like, learn to see the beauty in that person—because that is a person that God created and loves.*

*Since 8th grade I've dyed my hair, then when I started working in TV I wore tons of makeup, bleached my teeth and the sun spots on my skin, then fake-tanned my skin to make it look bronze, sculpted my eyebrows, the list goes on . . . but when I looked in the mirror at a bare face without product—I didn't see beauty.*

*Two weeks before we left to walk the Camino, I was in a hot yoga class where I was basically kicking my own butt physically. Toward the end of the class, I looked in the mirror to my bright red face and saw strength—and that was beautiful.*

*Now a week into my Camino, I had 30 minutes to spare in between a shower and a pilgrim's "welcome" at the church/albergue where we were staying. I laid in the grass and watched the trees sway in the wind. I took a picture of the trees then reversed the camera to gauge my thoughts about my appearance. I think I look at peace, and that, too, is beautiful.*

*Yesterday, I met a lovely couple from Ohio and the woman asked me to pick a card from her deck of scriptures. I closed my eyes and randomly chose the one that said, "Clothe yourselves . . . with the beauty that comes from within, the unfading beauty of a gentle and quiet spirit which is so precious to God." I Peter 3:4.*

*God is so sweet, and I appreciate examples of being given exactly what you need when you need it.*

# Jose

## Day 38

## Ventas de Narón, Galicia, Spain

In a twist of perspective, I've just learned that I earned two Lone Star Emmy Nominations in a place and at a time when my basic needs are not met. Today we sent a bag ahead that contained our sleeping gear, toothbrushes, other toiletry items, and our jackets. I always try to carry floss with me so at least I have partial peace where my teeth are concerned. I had eight cavities once as a kid and that must have traumatized me.

We sent a bag ahead to an amazing-looking albergue, but when we were about five kilometers away, we called them, and they were full. No room at the inn. We called another and then another, and no one had room. The spot where we paused to make the calls had openings, so—decision made.

We're staying put with plastic-like bed coverings that Peter just bought for two Euros, a slightly suspicious community blanket, and one backpack full of camera gear.

What an irony. As soon as I realized the predicament, I immediately got out my tripod, put on the big lens and started shooting beauty shots of lambs grazing across the street as the sun prepared to set. That big lens isn't going to brush these teeth though, or charge my phone, or keep me warm.

Materially, I just need a jacket and floss. I think that's all I really need for personal comfort. I'm sure it was no coincidence that right before I learned I had earned an Emmy nomination and right after I realized I only had camera gear to sleep with—Peter and I met Jose.

He's one of only a few people we have met from Texas and he is delightful. His gear is impeccable. Everything had a certain place and was well-organized and efficient. I was impressed.

In addition to his backpack, he wore a medium-sized pack on his front torso that contained his cellphone and pertinent items. It clipped on like a vest of sorts. Brilliant.

It didn't surprise me to learn that he's former-military. He started his Camino in Lourdes, France. I was a bit envious when he told us about his dip in the Holy waters where the Virgin Mary appeared 18 times in 1858.

Peter and I had planned to start our Camino in Lourdes, too, but when we arrived in Biarritz, we couldn't find any form of transportation to get us there because everything was locked down for the world leaders visiting the area for the G7 Summit.

I also appreciated hearing Jose's launch point because it was proof that he, too, is seeking something spiritually.

After we all chatted a bit, I asked him why he was walking. I've asked this question to almost everyone we've met who is willing to chat for more than a minute. The answers are varied. Some say it's just for the experience or that they like hiking, but others share much more.

I was grateful that Jose was willing to share, even though I saw on his face that he might not want me to pry too much. I do have a tendency to ask a lot of follow-up questions.

When I asked Jose why he was walking, his voice softened a bit and I noticed his head tilted slightly away from me. At that moment, the most beautiful Golden Retriever walked up to him out of nowhere and sat right next to him. (I just got full-body God bumps writing this.) Maybe the dog sensed that they both needed some support.

Jose said he spent 20-plus years in the military, served two tours overseas, his combat buddies had committed suicide (I'm not sure if it was one or several), and his marriage fell apart.

Perspective.

Jose has seen and dealt with more than I could ever imagine. He was also incredibly kind, outgoing, and just a lovely person to be around.

I think I met Jose when I did because I needed a broader perspective. I had just earned two nominations, but I was a bit disappointed that I didn't earn five. I was trying to remember which categories I had lost instead of being grateful for the ones that recognized my work. Writing about it now makes that concept seem ridiculous. Especially since that nomination can offer absolutely nothing helpful to me right now as I sit on plastic-ish sheets on the top bunk of a 10-bed community room in an albergue.

Now I'm just really glad I have this bed—it's cold outside.

# Competition

## *Day 38*

## *Ventas de Narón, Galicia, Spain*

My competitive spirit has been there as long as I can remember. Competing has always been fun when I've won— and I've won some random stuff. My memory is now recalling the moment I won a Pro-Am billiards tournament (with relatively no prior experience). I was paired with a professional pool player named Ewa "The Striking Viking" Laurance. She was so pretty. She told me where to hit the cue ball and how hard . . . and we won! At that time, I was learning about using energy to attract things. It certainly worked that night.

I won a road-rally competition at a CarMax car dealership grand opening once. The final leg of the competition had us packing boxes into the trunk of a Mustang. At that time, I drove a Mustang and was fully aware of the intricacies of its trunk—specifically how to fill the upper level first. I also decorated an outfit for the event. I bought a dark-blue Dickies jumpsuit (one that might be worn to paint a house) and I glued on flames, my last name, and other flare to get my competitive mojo going early. I won a lunchbox. I used it for years. I loved that lunchbox.

I was so proud—mostly of my outfit—and also beating the other TV people there who were all men and not at all impressed with my enthusiasm.

In college I rode horses for the Oklahoma State University Equestrian team. I remember doing the best when I was last to ride. I could watch everyone else do their pattern and I would know exactly what I needed to do better than them to win. A judge was the expert deciding, and there were many times I simply wasn't good enough. But by my fourth year on the team—I was good enough.

My senior year was (from what I can remember) the first time that I really put it all out there in the form of effort. At the end of the season, riders were allowed to keep practicing if they qualified to compete in regionals, nationals or extra competitions like the National Reining Horse Association Derby, which was for the top 12 college riders in the country who competed in a class called, "reining."

I was still competing. At times, it would get lonely at the barn at the end of a long, cold or wet day riding. I had a mantra that I'd say during those moments to keep me focused and motivated. It was, "leave nothing to chance." I was testing the idea that if I gave 100% in every moment of practice—not just riding, but lifting weights, running, eating clean—then in that ultimate test at the end, I would know that I did everything in my power to prepare. I would "leave nothing to chance."

That ultimate test came. I was riding in the Intercollegiate Horse Show Association Nationals and it was down to two riders for the overall winner of the western all-around, which is called the AQHA Cup. I was one of them.

The other rider and I had one more chance to do a reining pattern. The one who did the best, would be named national champion. It was an opportunity I had been actively working toward for four years, and an opportunity I had been preparing for since the first time I got on a horse with my grandfather's help. He would always have a great ranch horse for us, and we'd run them until we fell off (I'm sure the horses were grateful for the break).

At Nationals, going into that tie breaker, all of those experiences with countless horses, countless friends, my sister Kari who was my riding partner, they were all there with me. And I did it. I was able to do it because of them. I watched the other rider compete and she did fine, but I knew if I rode the heck out of that horse (meaning pushing it to go faster, stop harder, and spin without overstepping my mark) we'd win. The horse was willing and as soon as we finished our pattern, I knew we'd won. I gave it everything I had for so long and that effort was there for me to tap into when I needed it.

A similar situation happened not long after that competition, this time it was at the National Reining Horse Association Derby. I watched the returning champion ride his pattern, he had some bobbles, and I knew if I rode aggressively, we could win—and we did.

My test was proven successful. If I give every ounce of myself in effort, focus and willingness to do extra—I know that I can find success.

# In And Out Of TV-News

## Day 38

## Ventas de Narón, Galicia, Spain

I was grateful to see how my work ethic could easily translate to working in TV-news. It took some time though. At first, I was pretty lost as I tried to balance my work with my social life. Transitioning to be a real adult was a challenge—sans mandatory college-athlete workouts in the morning, being at the horse barn up to five hours in the afternoon, grade checks by my coach, etc. Yup, it took me a bit to find my inner motivator. But I knew I loved TV. The first day of my internship at Tulsa's Channel 8 I gave myself a bladder infection because I refused to take a break to go to the bathroom—there was too much to do and I just found it so exciting.

My intern boss used to force me to leave the building, which made me so frustrated because I just wanted to be in the building right in the middle of everything.

The transition out of TV-news was as clear as the transition into it, which happened in college. I was a business major taking a statistics class that was located in the journalism building. I was daydreaming and staring out the door when I saw a girl my age (wearing a business suit) run out the door. A moment later, another student followed her with a camera and tripod. I felt like my heart leapt out of my skin. I remember thinking, "Oh that looks like fun! I wonder what they are doing?"

That's what TV was for me for 15 years—fun. But after the miscarriage, it just seemed like I "felt" more. The breaking news stories, fires, car wrecks, murder investigations, Amber Alerts and kidnappings—they just seemed to weigh heavier on my spirit.

One day, I got a clear message from my intuition right in the middle of a newscast.

I was anchoring alone. We got to the second block of news, which is normally a bit happier. It's usually where you can find community events or feature stories that make you feel good. On this day, we did the opposite. The segment was filled with international stories of terrorism and mass casualties because of weather abroad.

This is the message that came to me, "I'm doing this wrong." I had an opportunity to share the best of humanity, but instead, I was sharing the worst.

Hearing in my head, "I'm doing this wrong," felt like a piece of my spirit was going to darken every time I continued to, "do this wrong."

I knew then, that if my inner-being was telling me I needed to share more positive content—then I needed to be the one to create it.

I had already told my boss that my time at NBC-5 would likely be coming to an end that summer, but now I was slowly getting more Divine nudges as to what's coming next. I knew I needed to prepare to capture goodness and to share the best of humanity, no longer the worst. I still had no idea how or where—I just knew I had to try.

My biggest challenge? How do I prepare for a "national championship" if I don't even know what the "competition" is? Having an end-goal makes it easier to backtrack and visualize the steps to get there. As of this moment, my life goal is to love God and be happy. So, does this mean that for the first time in 20 years I am working toward a goal that doesn't involve a trophy, a promotion, a raise, or a free lunchbox from CarMax?

How do I "leave nothing to chance" in this situation? Is it meditating extra, loving extra, showing kindness and empathy extra? How do I know if I'm doing it well enough or making any progress at all because I don't have benchmarks or yearly reviews from a boss?

In theory, my new boss is God, my immediate supervisor is my Guru. If I receive a letter in the mail from either of them regarding company benefits, I'm going to flip my lid.

# Tatjana

## *Day 39*

## *Ponte Campaña, Galicia, Spain*

At the end of eating a family-style dinner at our albergue tonight, I sat staring intensely into the plastic tablecloth as my brain processed a gift of advice that came from our new German friend Tatjana. She sat down across from us to chat—even though she wasn't eating.

This was the second time today we had unexpectedly bumped into her. The first time was when Peter and I turned off the main trail to take a short walk up to a café. Tatjana happened to be the only person sitting outside the restaurant. When we tried to go inside—the door was locked. So, we chatted briefly, then Peter and I continued our search for our second breakfast of the day.

When it comes to finding a bed for the night, there are between one and a dozen or so albergues in each town, depending on its size. So, when we randomly choose one and find a familiar face already there—it is a lovely surprise.

Tatjana is always a treat to see. She's reserved in what she says, but she's a character. Her short, spiky grey hair is balanced with big gold hoop earrings that don't match and bright blue eyes. When she smiles, sometimes I detect a hint of mischief, which is great.

Peter and I keep bumping into her. I've learned on this Camino, that I will keep randomly bumping into someone until I have learned whatever it is that I need to learn from them—and then they're gone.

Unfortunately, that means I likely won't see Tatjana again after tonight.

Out of our 35 days walking, we've bumped into her at least five different days, sometimes twice a day, making her the person we've seen the most often (I think).

Her lessons have been about money and attachment to money. I am quite attached. My mom said I was born that way. She said when I was little, I saved my money and finally decided to buy a Barbie. After much consideration, I purchased the doll at our local mall. Immediately after I bought it, I broke into tears and wanted my money back. I apparently said, "I don't want that stupid doll," because I'd rather have the money. That pretty much sums me up.

Also as a child, we raised various animals in the youth organization 4-H. The goal was to feed and work with the animals for around five months, then we'd compete with them at the local fair. If we placed well enough in the competition, we got to sell our animals at the fair's livestock auction (to really nice people or generous businesses who wanted to support youth in livestock). My grandparents had a competitive rabbit showing/breeding operation in their retirement—so needless to say we usually made the sale with our rabbits.

Since elementary school, I was in charge of feeding our rabbits for the fair, grooming their coats and practicing with them to sit still to be judged. The rabbits were the Californian breed, which came with white bodies and black ears and tails. The goal was when the judge posed them, the rabbits would be relaxed, have fur that was soft and fell back into place when petting the opposite direction, and their muscles and frame should feel like running your hand over a basketball.

There was never a year (out of about ten years as a youth 4-Her) that I did not make the sale.

I still have that rabbit money.

It contributed to my down payment on my first house, then my second house, and now it's sitting in the bank with hopes I'll never have to touch it.

For me, the hardest part of leaving a career was leaving a paycheck that was deposited into my bank account every two weeks and a paper version arrived in the mail to confirm it.

I made the mistake once of saying out loud, "I could never not work for someone, I enjoy a consistent paycheck too much." Tests. I feel like I brought on this test with that sentence alone.

Not having money is a legit fear of mine. When I would transfer money from my checking to my savings account there would be a positive physical response. It literally would feel good in my core to save money. To me, it's safety, it's potential, it's the results of effort and work that I can stare at via online banking.

It was made clear in numerous ways that I needed to leave my job at NBC-5—even though it was a safe and predictable income, and a skill I knew how to do because I'd spent 15 years working to perfect the craft.

But how was I going to survive without any foreseeable income? Because I definitely don't want to tap into that rabbit money.

About a week or two ago, we walked through a small village and saw Tatjana sitting at a café. We stopped to sit down with her because it was getting a bit awkward bumping into her so much and not talking.

She randomly said, "money doesn't just come from working." I had to think about that for a while.

I had somehow forgotten about the law of attraction and most importantly—the words that people kept mentioning to me as I shared the early plans for this journey: If God provides the vision, He will provide the provision.

# $1.91

## *Day 39*

## *Ponte Campaña, Galicia, Spain*

"If God provides the vision, He will provide the provision," brought me to tears while sitting in a Bank of America in Las Cruces, New Mexico. It was the moment we opened a checking account for our video production company that Peter and I created before leaving for the Camino.

Months before, I knew I needed to upgrade my camera so I could record our faith walk in 4K. The total bill would be thousands of dollars and my income from NBC-5 would be coming to an end. So, any money taken from our savings (including a partially cashed-out 401K) to pay for gear would be money not available for our travels.

Each time I thought about the expense it was clear—I have to shoot in 4K. The importance of 4K is basically how big of a screen (movie theater screen vs television screen) can be used to watch our work. I don't know the end-goal here, but I know I don't want to limit God's plan by being cheap.

So, I spent around $7,000 on new camera gear.

Not long after I spent the money, I got a text from my first TV-production internship boss asking me to help her with a horse-focused television show. She'd been hired at the last minute to produce it and she needed someone to be on camera who knew about horses.

We were also forced to meet a wonderful man who needed a video made about his county's Veterans Memorial. He and his volunteer partner said building the memorial was the most important thing they'd ever done—both men are in their late 70s or 80s.

So, odd jobs like these popped up and we didn't think much about it—even though Peter, nor I, had ever been given freelance work in a decade—that was until I was sitting in that Bank of America in Las Cruces.

My mom had driven us to the bank to meet the local-business representative so we could open an account with the checks we had from the extra projects. Peter wrote out the deposit slip and totaled the final number using his cell phone's calculator. Out of curiosity, I pulled up my credit card bill online while I sat there to remind myself of exactly how much I spent on the camera gear. I looked at my bill. I looked at our bank deposit slip. I looked again. The difference was $1.91.

For days, I thought of that number. How did God do that? And so exact? But using so many different people over so much time to have a difference of $1.91. But why $1.91?

Then my curiosity (and lack of knowledge of biblical scriptures) had me Googling "scripture 1-9-1," and there it was. The scripture that my mentor Yvonne had given me almost a year before: Psalm 91:4 (NIV). He will cover you with his feathers, and under his wings you will find refuge; his faithfulness will be your shield and rampart.

Remembering $1.91 is part of why I was intensely staring off into the plastic table cover that night, because it was all coming together.

I had thought my Camino would be filled with deep conversations about God, faith and religious perspective, but

I wasn't even close. It's so much bigger than that. So much deeper.

It's the people you meet along the way and the lessons they teach you. God, working through people and pairing those pilgrims, volunteers and locals who create the "magic" of the Camino—is on a Spiritual level so much deeper than I ever could have expected or hoped for. Each pilgrim is strategically meeting, conversing, and truly hearing exactly what they need in order to more fully live their life.

So, when Tatjana sat down in front of me at dinner, which had three rows of tables set up like a horseshoe with seats only on the outside, Tatjana created her own space on the inside. She started sharing with me about trusting God to provide, and I will know to trust Him because of my own experiences.

She said for her, as soon as the fear (of not having enough money and living under a bridge) did not exist, then her needs were always met. She said in order to release the fear, you simply have to be present. Because if you're focused on exactly what is happening right now in front of you, anxiety or fear of the future in the form of worrying is impossible.

As I'm writing this, I'm remembering being told to "be present, be positive, live in the now," but listening with an inner eye roll. I have no expectations that this will be easy.

# Confirmation
## (One Month Later)

### Day 63
### Ranchi, Jharkhand, India

There are so many great prayers to aid in God providing our needs, we just need to ask. We also need to believe deep down that whatever it is we want, already belongs to us—like we are the children of Divine royalty who "already own" everything there is to want, we just have to ask for it. When I ask, I put forth my full heart energy in the prayer—feeling a subtle vibration that starts in my heart and spreads to my entire body, the room around me, the country I'm in, the earth, and then beyond. I then try to see the object I'm trying to receive; I feel it, I experience it. I infuse energy in that same process for any style of prayer.

I learned one law-of-attraction prayer from a Native American couple, one of which was a healer when he was younger. They said when the moon is full, raise your hands up toward it and say several times, "Grandpa, fill up my pockets."

There is also a simple, yet powerful, prayer that Yvonne taught me, "Release what is owed." It's basically a call to the universe to release any money or gifts that might be overdue, forgotten about, or tied up for any unknown reason. I prayed, "Release what is owed," several times on the Camino after having the money conversation with Tatjana.

A month after my conversation with her, when she reminded me that money doesn't just come from work, I received an email from a title company in Texas. I used their services when I almost bought a house in Grapevine. The sale fell through after the appraisal, which left me frustrated and rushed to find a new place for us to live. I hadn't thought about that title company since, until they sent me this email:

*"Hi Kristin. If you remember our office had a transaction for you to purchase the above property back in 2016. It has come to my attention in the setting of the audit that the $3,500 you deposited was never refunded to you when the contract was cancelled. I understand that you may be traveling out of the country. I will be sending you a Docusign Release of Earnest Money, if you will please open the link and sign. I also need instructions where you want us to send the check. We are hoping to get these funds released today to satisfy our audit."*

Just like that, an unexpected $3,500 was deposited into my bank account. How did I forget about that money? For being such a stickler with cash, I was surprised I let it slip by. But that prayer, "release what is owed" worked on my behalf to release money I didn't even know I was owed. Tatjana said I should trust that God will provide because of my own experiences. She was right.

# Luggage Karma

## *Day 39*

## *Ponte Campaña, Galicia, Spain*

While staring at the tablecloth, my brain processed the complex series of connections between what Tatjana was saying and what I've already learned. It brought up a brief memory of my "luggage karma." Four times in a row, while flying within the US and internationally, the airlines lost or misplaced my luggage. The first time it happened, I was in-country. I called and yelled at some poor woman at the airline. I was furious. Then it kept happening to me. What's the deal? After the second or third time my luggage got lost, I realized it might be happening to teach me a lesson, and it would keep happening until I learned that lesson.

So, I started working on not being attached to material goods. I also needed to work on being emotionally stable when frustrations or challenges are happening all around me. Having a quiet heart in all circumstances was my new goal.

A poem on this very issue came to me. Canon T.T. Carter wrote it and we framed two copies—one for work and one at home.

> *"Humility is perpetual quietness of heart. It is to have no trouble. It is never to be fretted, or vexed, or irritated, or sore, or disappointed. It is to expect nothing, to wonder at nothing that is done to me, to feel nothing done against me. It is to be at rest when nobody praises me, and when I am blamed and*

*despised. It is to have a blessed home in myself, where I can go in and shut the door, and kneel to my father in secret, and be at peace as in a deep sea of calmness when all around and above is troubled."*

This poem was my new life goal, something to work toward.

So, when my luggage was lost a fourth time, which was the second time it was lost while flying into India, it didn't faze me. All was calm within and outside me. I even shared a chai with the Indian airport's employees as they took their break before sorting out my problem.

The poem helped, and not one of my bags has been misplaced since.

It was a similar situation for Tatjana. She said for her, as soon as she stopped worrying about money—as soon as she released control and was not physically affected by her concern—she hasn't had a problem since.

During the end of our conversation with Tatjana, I thought about the first time we met her.

Peter and I were in the middle of a pretty strenuous hike through the mountains. There was a bench at one lookout toward the top. On that bench, Peter found a brown fleece jacket. It was tiny. The size was a lady's extra small.

We had already seen a few items along the Camino that people either lost or left behind. I figured someone left the brown fleece behind because they no longer needed it in the mountains. Peter disagreed and decided to attach the fleece to the outside of his pack so the person who forgot it might see it. He carried it for about two-and-a-half hours, finally leaving it outside a restaurant in the first town after the mountain hike.

We ate lunch and continued walking for another hour. The skies started sprinkling with a light rain, so we stopped in a small village's only albergue to sit down and contemplate our plan to either keep walking or stop for the day.

Tatjana was staying inside that albergue. She was enjoying a hot tea on the back patio, but all of a sudden, she felt a cool breeze and came out front to where I was sitting. Peter had just walked away to offer an elderly man his medical kit because the man was cleaning his feet with a white cloth and it looked like he was bleeding.

When Peter returned, Tatjana was sitting in his seat. She complimented me on my hat. I explained that Peter found two feathers and wove them into the hat's crown (feathers being a reminder of God).

I told her my hat was actually Peter's to begin with, I'd misplaced my hat before leaving for the Camino only to find it in a side zipper in my backpack—I'd unknowingly been carrying it for two weeks.

She said she, too, misplaced something: her brown fleece jacket. She sat on it on a mountain-top bench then walked off and forgot it.

What are the chances? Tatjana was missing her jacket, then got to meet the very person trying to return it—all thanks to a cool breeze that moved her out of the back of the albergue and right into Peter's seat.

How does God do it?

This taught me that I need to more actively look for Him working through people—on the Camino and in life.

My next task is trusting in Him that if I'm following His lead, then He will provide. Because unlike the luggage, I don't want to have to learn a financial lesson four times.

# Camino Music

## *Day 39*

## *Ponte Campaña, Galicia, Spain*

That night, after eating numerous rounds of food including vegetable stew, salad, Spanish tortilla, potatoes and green beans with carrots, stewed beef, ice cream cake and a yellow Santiago cake with powdered sugar on top—one of our fellow pilgrims from Italy walked around the horseshoe-shaped row of tables to grab a guitar from the corner of the room. This was only the second time during our Camino when dessert was followed by a community of walkers joining together in song.

The first time was after a tour of a church, which was modeled after Paris' Notre Dame. The acoustics in one of the church's chambers were too good not to be taken advantage of.

Each time, the songs were mostly spiritual—maybe because of the intent of the trip for many people, or maybe it's because songs like Hallelujah and Amazing Grace are known well enough by people from a variety of countries who speak various languages.

The first song on this night stood out. It had significance to me, my Camino, and the transformation that I'm slowly seeing and also hoping for. The first song played was also the song I heard after waking up in Zabaldika. I had just dreamed of dying in a car wreck and then saw hands enter my body to bring me back to life. The song is Bob Dylan's "Like a Rolling

Stone." I don't yet fully understand its relationship to me, but I hope to soon. The chorus is "how does it feel . . . to be on your own, with no direction home, like a complete unknown, like a rolling stone."

# Love Bubbles

## *Day 41*

## *Muxía, Galicia, Spain*

Peter calls them "love bubbles." He pointed out that I've had them every other day or every third day while walking the Camino. To me, a love bubble feels like an almost overwhelming feeling of love, gratitude and God's presence in the form of inner-peace.

Peter also says I often have them before eating. In my defense, that also means we've just walked a bunch and we are starting to take a break.

I had a love bubble as we sat down at a well-reviewed restaurant in Muxía. I was just so grateful. So, instead of starting to eat our first course of salad with pineapple, local prawns, a mayo-like aioli and balsamic reduction in addition to a white-wine vinaigrette dressing—I closed my eyes, embraced the feelings and silently told God how much I love and appreciate Him. So much love.

I thought about all the people that He has surrounded me with throughout my life—family, parents, sisters, grandparents, friends—all of which have poured love into me. And when there were challenges, He too, surrounded me with people who could help me through them.

I often wouldn't realize the significance of the help, nor the challenge, until long after it was over.

When I broke down and cried in the Meseta, I was thinking about how close Peter and I came to our marriage failing and how I almost let one person bring us to that point—Peter's dad.

After sitting down and crying, it was in the getting up and continuing to walk that an opposite thought and emotion came—gratitude. I thought about Yvonne. She's a certified counselor, pastor, and she's the only person who we'll both listen to. She rescued us.

It took a solid year-and-a-half, but she rescued us. As I walked, my sorrow turned to prayers of gratitude. How thoughtful that God gave me that friendship, and also whispered in her ear to check on us at key moments.

I once read a theory about memories. Why is it that if 100 people tell you something nice, but only one person tells you something mean—you remember the mean and forget about the nice? The theory, which seems like fact to me, is that the strength of the memory is based on how much energy you put toward it. So if the mean comment has a physical reaction to your emotions, you think about it over and over, each time getting just as frustrated—that memory is going to stick with you more than the nice comment that you brush off and don't think about again.

So, after that moment in the Meseta, I realized I need to change the power of these memories. Now, when Peter's dad comes to mind, I'm going to think about Yvonne—her support, her love, her time, her patience, her kind and supportive words, and her strength to choose us and keep pouring into us as friends.

I'll also think of my mom. She told me once that she had a plan to fly to our house in Texas, pull Peter's dad aside, hand him a one-way plane ticket and a thousand dollars in cash to get out of my life. I loved her so much for that plan—and I'd love her without it. But my mom knew that challenge was something Peter and I had to deal with as a couple.

Maybe six months after she told me her idea, we did a version of it. We sold our house—forcing our overdue roommate to leave the building. We gave him Peter's car, $300 in cash and a credit card to use for a few months while he got settled in Florida.

Challenges always make you stronger, but so often, it sucks getting stronger. It's kind of like I want to have sculpted legs, but I don't want to go to the gym because it's hard.

That muscle also exists in your emotions, your patience, your love, your faith. Countless tests fill our lives and it's up to us to choose to allow them to make us stronger, to learn from them, and be better.

# Santiago's Gifts

## *Day 42*

## *Muxía, Galicia, Spain*

Our walk into Santiago could not have been more special. Yes, we already finished and now we're celebrating by doing anything but walking. I'm sitting in a small apartment with a window that faces the harbor in Muxía. The end of town is also the end of land—a quick walk lets you see water in nearly all directions. The harbor has local fishing boats—half were working hard today while the others looked like they haven't moved in a bit.

Today we walked to the town's supermarket and bought a melon—one of our favorite local fruits of Spain. Its flavor is similar to a ripe honeydew and its green flesh is crisp and delicious—often served with thinly-sliced cured pork. Peter just learned the melon is called the "Santa Claus melon," and what a gift it was.

The first time we ate it on the Camino, it was my birthday. We started walking super early that day to shoot video of the sunrise at Alto del Perdon. Afterward, we celebrated our productivity by brunching for almost four hours. I started breakfast with dessert because that's what you do when it's your birthday.

So, celebrating the end of the walk with fruit is fitting because fruit has been a special offering throughout this time in nature. There was the apple tree the first day hiking—when we realized we weren't as physically prepared as we thought we were. That tree provided us several flawless apples that waited for us on the ground as we took a much-needed break half-way up the mountain. We offered one to Laura as she sat down with us and she returned the offering with nuts. It was our first pilgrim picnic and that apple tree was to credit.

Fruit blows my mind in a "how does it even work" kind of way. Fruit trees take nutrients from the soil, then its wood texture gives birth to something that tastes incredible and can easily be stored—like it's created with its own to-go bag in mind. Incredible.

So, as we ventured toward Santiago, we were always on the lookout for an apple tree that might offer us a treat in the form of a fallen fruit that was still in good shape. We could have easily picked one from a tree, but we knew that the apples likely belonged to someone who might be trying to sell them.

That first tree was the only one we ate from for free. As we walked the last kilometer before seeing the city of Santiago, the mist and clouds created a really shallow visibility for us. I felt like I was walking through a cool shower. We could see roughly 40 yards ahead of us and not much to either side.

As we stared up a paved black street, we saw a green apple rolling down the road toward us. It stopped at Peter's feet. He picked it up. It only had one small nick on it from where it hit the ground moments before. It didn't even have time to bruise before we could bite into it. What a delicious gift.

When we bought our home in Texas, Peter planted ten fruit trees and vines in our backyard. I saw it as an early commitment to my new employer because those trees weren't expected to bear fruit for three to five years. We had no idea that we'd only be living in that home for two years.

Our third year was spent in an apartment. Someone from China bought our house and turned it into a rental.

Peter loved those plants equally and invested a substantial amount of time researching the best fruit, the farms where they started their lives, and how he could help them succeed in Texas. We later took personality tests and found out Peter's personal satisfaction comes from seeing small amounts of growth in other people, plants, or in this case, fruit trees.

I was especially looking forward to the kiwis he planted in our yard. Peter built a trellis for them, adjusted the soil and checked them daily to assess their growth and help them latch onto their supports. He was never able to witness them succeed at bearing fruit.

Right after we indulged in the green apple that rolled to Peter's feet, we, for the first time ever, saw kiwis growing on a vine. They were living at a home that backed up to the road. It had at least four well-established kiwi plants that looked like an ancient vineyard of grapes. It was an astonishing sight to finally see the results of something we put in the ground as twigs—even if these results were happening in someone else's yard on the other side of the world.

One of the tastiest surprises on our Camino was finding wild blackberry plants along the trail—from start to finish. Hiking up that first hill to leave Saint-Jean-Pied-de-Port, we stopped for a breather and a blackberry quite often.

Then, right before we went down the steps to descend into Santiago, we saw a bush full of ripe blackberries. It seemed like they were ready and waiting to tell the tired and excited pilgrims, "good job!" and maybe even hoping to hear in return, "thank you for your help along the way."

Today I asked Peter, "What was your biggest surprise along the Camino?" Sometimes I expect a philosophical answer, but Peter can be quite logical. For example, one of the first gifts he ever gave me was an electric toothbrush. I found it an interesting choice, but then I used it twice a day for several years, proving it was a perfect and incredibly thoughtful gift. So, when I asked him about any Camino surprises, I shouldn't have been surprised by his answer. He said, "I'm surprised that all of the cafés had an espresso machine and a high-quality juicer for orange juice." Solid point. The coffee seemed less caffeinated than we were used to drinking, but the juice was absolutely incredible, and it was available anywhere. Even in the smallest of towns, we'd walk into the only cafe and there would be a box of ripe oranges and a giant juicer. Yum.

Most pilgrims' breakfasts on a fixed menu included coffee, fresh orange juice and toast. So, as we were halfway through the city of Santiago and nearing the cathedral, I took a pitstop for one last orange juice. Honestly, I really only needed to use the restroom and I felt better about going inside to use the facilities if I bought something.

Peter placed the order for a juice while I found the door that said "aseos." We'd be back on the road in no time. I came out and found our drinks with a spread of food—bread, ham, various chorizo slices, cheese and freshly-fried potato chips. I thought, "Peter got a case of the snackies." He said, "No. I ordered the drinks and the rest just showed up."

I had a love bubble—and yes, as Peter pointed out, that overwhelming feeling of love and gratitude once again came before food. For the first time I realized—we made it. We walked across a country (while also utilizing a horse, a taxi, a train and sometimes Peter pushing me from behind), but we made it.

I thought about how we were Divinely taken care of by countless people along the way offering us advice, support and guidance either about what to eat, where to sleep or how to better live our lives. We were given love and support from sweet animals along the path—horses letting me get close for a nose scratch, dogs coming to sit down at just the right moment, even a pair of swans flying over us and leading the way toward a lake on the path. Then there was nature providing for us in the form of fruits growing along the Camino—feeding countless pilgrims for more than 10 centuries.

For some reason, the free bar snacks put me over the edge. My capacity to accept love was full, and I still am just so very grateful. Grateful to God for allowing us to do this, grateful to my body for being willing to keep going just a little bit farther, grateful to Peter for being an incomparable travel partner, and grateful for all the people at home sending us love and support.

We did it, but we still weren't actually there yet. Peter pushed through tendon pain in his left shin and ankle, the rain and mist never seemed to stop, but the markers telling us where to go did stop (or at least we lost track of them). Google Maps might have taken us the longest way possible to the cathedral. We finally walked into the square from a side entrance right at 8:30 that night. We had started walking that morning around 9.

The rain and mist and the late hour created a perfect setting for our final steps. There were maybe a dozen people in the square (compared to the hundreds that were there 18 hours later). It was quiet and still with only the sound of someone playing a bagpipe in an archway around the corner. There was no big celebration, just a humble welcome by an ancient cathedral currently closed for renovation. It was perfect.

# Make It Your Camino

## *Day 43*

## *Muxía, Galicia, Spain*

From very early on in our Camino planning, countless people told us, "Make it your Camino," which I interpreted as, "do the best you can and do it the way you want to do it."

Sometimes it might take a few days for someone to find their best walking pace that balances any distance-goal for the day, their body's ability to do it and then recover from it, and what time they want to be done walking. We met two sweet women from Canada who had their schedule down perfectly. They started walking at sunup and got to their albergue by 1-ish in the afternoon, showered, drank wine or beer, had an early dinner before the restaurants closed for siesta, then relaxed all night. Since their schedule was predictable, they were able to reserve a bed at an albergue ahead of time, which became a necessity for the last 100 kilometers because so many people joined the Camino for that last section.

The last 100 kilometers are also the only ones that "count" at the official pilgrim's office where they award you a certificate called a Compostela when you finish. If you don't speak kilometers, which I still struggle with, 100 kilometers is 62.137 miles.

During our Camino, we walked roughly 380 miles, but as of this writing, we did not apply for a Compostela. Several pilgrims told us they waited in line for four hours to get their piece of paper noting their accomplishment. I don't know if we need that paper to remind us what we did. Or do we? There is also a bit of hesitation because we jumped forward a handful of times during our five-and-a-half weeks walking— including during that last 100 kilometers.

Galicia is known for unpredictable weather. We were constantly walking in the rain with only a few moments of sun or dry skies. On what would be our final day walking toward Santiago, we jumped on a bus after lunch to get out of the rain. As we boarded the bus, my face lit up with a smile and my hands automatically started silently clapping. We'd found them! Sitting there with two open seats nearby, was a family from Barbados that we chatted with briefly while staying in an albergue together in León. I was walking to my bed and a young boy popped his head out from the lower bunk next to Peter. His eyes were bright, and his excitement level was a full 100%. He said he spoke three languages (English, German and Spanish), this was his fourth or fifth (partial) Camino, and he was 14 years old. In amazement, I asked, "Who are you here with? Are you walking alone?" "No!" he said in an "of course not" kind of tone. "I'm with my family," all seven of them. He is the oldest of five children and they are all walking 300 or so kilometers together to get to Santiago.

My mind was blown. It was hard enough for me and Peter to organize ourselves with nightly laundry washing, choosing a place to stay, finding food and carrying water for some long stretches of bare countryside. I couldn't imagine being organized enough to walk the Camino with five children, one of which was younger than two. But they were doing it and were incredibly good at it. The kids are all home-schooled, well-spoken, curious, kind, and every time we saw them, they looked very happy to be there.

Seeing them on the bus was the third of four times we would bump into them, and it was the first time we'd be able to ask them about their story. The parents met as missionaries and now do spiritual work in Barbados, including offering classes on prayer and meditation to better experience God. They said that after walking the Camino they would spend one month in Galicia to pray for that region and its people. Incredible.

The mom said it is a region that has experienced a lot of pain over the centuries from war and fighting over religion. She said the remnants of that pain can be seen today—one way is the weather, which is often dreary. Our conversation with that family was several days ago.

As of this writing, the family has been actively praying for Galicia while staying here on the coast the last two days. Both days have been sunny and beautiful.

# Filling The Hole

## *Day 43*

## *Lires, Galicia, Spain*

We just left the beautiful town of Muxía, which I just learned sounds like Moo-she-uh, and we arrived at the equally-beautiful Lires (sounds like Lee-des). Lires is half-way to Finisterre and is also located on the coast.

We are staying at a family-run boutique hotel called Casa Raul. Our room's walls are made of large rocks that are a brownish-cream color. It feels like it's provided housing and comfort for people for centuries. The blanket on the bed is also cream with stitches like the final ones on a quilt that attach the hand-work to the soft underside.

In the taxi on the way here, it got a bit warm. I also might be feeling a touch of Peter's head cold, so my body was not comfortable. The conditions brought back a memory from my mid-20s (before I met Peter).

I woke up on a bright sunny morning in the back of a cab. The driver was yelling at me saying I owed him $200. Of course, he must be wrong, I thought; even though I had no idea how I got there or just how long I'd been in his cab. I was in a city that wasn't my home and I was very confused.

I refused to pay him the $200 so he drove me to a police station. An officer came to check in, I gave up arguing and paid the driver with a credit card. I saw a hotel close by, walked in and told the receptionist and a man speaking with her that I was in a mess. The man was the hotel's shuttle driver. They both took pity on me, thank God.

I was outside of Seattle in a suburb. The night before, we had gone into the city to celebrate while reuniting with my best friends (and AP English study group) from high school. We had a great time, but somehow, I missed the ferry, got arrested, and was sent to the drunk tank for being intoxicated in public. The shuttle driver helped me find the address to where I could find my friends. I arrived there safely, and the shuttle driver and I remained acquaintances on Facebook.

When I walked inside to my friend's home, I realized I smelled like vomit, but before I cleaned up, we all ate warm tortillas and had a tremendous laugh at the ridiculousness of the last 18 hours. We were still alive by the grace of God.

Why did I have to test that grace? What was I trying to escape? I'm so glad I quit drinking. I'm so glad I met Jen on the Camino who reminded me I still "don't have to drink."

I realize now that I used to drink to fill a hole within myself.

After we got settled into our room in Lires, Peter and I took a short walk to the Cabanas da Ría Eco-resort for lunch.

If we ever get to go back to Spain, spending a week at this resort and eating their food every day would be a top priority.

From our table in the dining room, I looked up and into the kitchen and saw my salad being made. American music was playing overhead and the sweet woman working on my lunch was dancing while adding the final layers of goat cheese and walnuts. The song she was dancing to was Rod Stewart's "Ooh La La" and the lyrics were right on time, "I wish that I knew what I know now, when I was younger."

Finding God and feeling His peace filled that hole, and as it happened, the temporary fillers like alcohol slowly started to release their hold on me.

# Drama-Free Zone

## *Day 44*

## *Lires, Galicia, Spain*

Nearly four weeks into walking the Camino, I realized that I had absolutely no drama in my life. I took a break from Twitter during our three-month pilgrimage hiatus, so hourly updates of news and people's opinions about it were not in my mind. On Instagram and Facebook, I was only responding to comments made on our Camino posts and thank God they were all positive. I was texting a few friends and family members who were all really quiet about their personal lives and only offered us support. It was a lovely bubble to be in. I told Peter, "we are drama free!" Saying that was mistake number one and it created a learning opportunity for me based on the events that followed.

We came down from a long mountain hike that was challenging because of its rocky footing. This was the same mountain where Peter carried Tatjana's brown fleece. When we arrived in the next town, we were beyond ready for some lunch and a break from walking. We picked a restaurant that had "crepes" written on its sidewalk sign, which was a big change from the regular pilgrims' menu.

We sat at a table inside near the front door. There were only a few tables inside and we later realized the main seating area was a patio around the corner. Not sitting outside was our second mistake. As we sat there, we had a front-row seat to witness the heat in the kitchen.

There was a woman cooking who was around our age and spoke several languages. She seemed to have everything together, but her male manager would come into the kitchen after working the cash register (because no other employee, including our waitress, was allowed to touch any money) and he appeared to completely throw things in disarray.

They'd start yelling at each other, pointing fingers in each other's faces, all maybe five feet away from us. I immediately took her side thinking, "She doesn't deserve this." She made us amazing salads, so we figured she was awesome at her job.

The mean manager in this situation could actually be amazing, but maybe we just saw him on his worst day ever; however, restaurant reviewers on Google Maps also noted yelling in the kitchen during busy hours and for any potential customers to avoid the restaurant.

We sat there for what felt like two hours—yelling, chaos, more yelling—what a mess. We should've left long before ever placing an order—and that was our final mistake.

Before we left, the manager was busy making a latte. Peter gave me 10 Euros and I snuck over to the lady in the kitchen. From what we've found, tipping isn't expected in Spain. If we leave a two Euro coin, the server will usually refuse it twice before finally taking it.

The woman was kneeling down, and I showed her the bill and whispered, "good luck." I put my hand on her shoulder and when I did, I felt either her pain or a memory of my own. It felt like an exhausting, "I'm stuck, out of options, and in a total mess" kind of pain. I nearly cried as I was barely able to say it one more time, "good luck."

The worst part of the situation was that her mean manager was from Dallas—the city we left. The only person we had seen from our former home happened to be the worst one. Again, I'm sure he's had better days, but dang.

As we walked down the hill away from the restaurant, Peter and I talked about the wreck-of-a-workplace we just witnessed. Should we go back and yell at that guy? Should we tell him he needs to treat his female employees better? Or tell him he should take a management class to learn how to prevent raging fights in front of customers?

We decided that there was little benefit to us yelling at him, but we could cause a risk of retaliation that could make the female employee's situation even worse—so we kept walking.

Not far after, I saw the first (and only) snake on the Camino ground. I actively look for snakes because they scare me and when I thought I was seeing them on the trail it would always be a squiggly-shaped root or twig—never a snake sighting, until now.

It was a tiny black snake and it appeared harmless because of its size. And that's where the perspective came in. The intimidation was all in appearance. It couldn't hurt anyone, but it sure could scare someone.

Was the manager big and intimidating? Or harmless? It was all in how you saw him.

To me, the snake also represented someone from my past, a former boss. He was a snake with an unsuspecting bite in the form of words. He had the ability to read people and tell them exactly what they needed to hear in order to get what he wanted out of them. Man, did it work on me. I once told someone, "I'd lay in traffic for the guy." It was the opposite of a snake charmer, because the snake was the charmer. His eyes also sparkled in a way that I could never tell if he was looking directly at me or to the side of me. Tricky and unsettling. Countless people fell victim and some likely didn't know they were not alone.

My former boss was also similar to the restaurant manager coming into the kitchen and making things difficult just for the sake of mixing things up. He thrived on drama. If there wasn't enough naturally, he'd pit two co-workers against each other and sit back to watch the unnecessary stress. Who does that? Why would you want to work for someone who likes to put people on edge for no reason? I personally don't work well when my surroundings are insecure, not supportive, and unpredictable.

I love working hard for people and often the best payment is a verbal, "good job," or just a simple sign of recognition that implies, "I see you." I have had countless amazing managers who are still friends; however, the snake might have taught me the biggest lessons. I learned a lot about myself and the strength of peer support, but those lessons were the most painful to learn.

So, the snake in my life, the restaurant manager, and then this tiny black snake on the ground looking helpless. The lesson for me was tied together by one more event that happened while walking to dinner that night.

We were looking at a menu outside a restaurant debating whether we wanted to eat there. A woman with a high, black ponytail walked by us to enter and took a long drag of a cigarette. Her skin was tight and tanned and she was followed by a really big guy who spends a lot of time in the gym. As she started to exhale smoke toward the sky, the guy grabbed her by her ponytail and pulled her head back. I said this in my mind, and I might have mumbled it out loud, "oh f—no." As I mouthed it, I glanced down from the couple and made eye contact with a young boy with them who was roughly 12 years old. I just got busted for cussing, but there was no way I was going to spend any more time that day witnessing unhealthy and potentially abusive relationships.

I also felt for the young boy. Will he see these two adults as role models in how to treat a woman? By completely dominating her by pulling her by the hair? What lesson was I supposed to learn here?

I started the day pointing out how drama-free our lives were, then I was basically forced to witness two very dramatic relationships (topped off with a snake) in the course of two meals.

Here's the lesson I took away from the day: I saw the restaurant manager and the ponytail-puller as a reminder that I always have a choice about who I surround myself with. In the restaurant, the woman cooking was skilled and could work elsewhere. The ponytail girl didn't have to be treated that way. I don't know their full stories, but it served as this reminder to me: I have a choice.

Avoiding drama is a choice. The smallest form for me of avoiding drama is attempting to reduce the drama I see and hear. I rarely watch fictional TV shows anymore because they affect my emotions and my time. I've done my best to avoid watching talk shows where people argue for any or no reason. If relationships don't make me feel positive and uplifted, I'm going to end them (or avoid them) much sooner. First sign of it—I'm out. These are all hard things I try to do, because I need to choose me, my sanity, and my happiness.

# My Path To God

## *Day 45*

## *Fisterra (Finisterre), Galicia, Spain*

God is so sweet. I knew for a few days now that the next thing I needed to write about was my journey to finding Him. How on earth do I start? What should I say? What if people judge me? Then this morning happened. He was so sweet to give so much thoughtfulness into His chapter, but aren't all of these chapters His?

Before traveling to Fisterra, Peter and I were enjoying our fifth meal in three days at Cabanas da Ría's restaurant in Lires. It's our new happy place. The food is amazing and the café con leches are the best in Spain. It also has the appearance of a brightly colored island resort equipped with tiki huts and a hammock. Lires is a magical place. From our table on the restaurant's patio, we can see everything Lires has to offer.

We have a view of the mountains that are covered with pine and eucalyptus trees. Below them, two rivers converge into the ocean and seem to tussle when the tide comes in or goes out. Bob Marley is playing in the background. I hear the lyric, "You can't forget your past," from his song "No Woman, No Cry."

The woman serving us food is named Sonia. She said she grew up in a town down the road from Lires, but spent eleven years in the UK, so she has a beautiful British accent to go with her Spanish descent. When she's not smiling, she looks just like my oldest sister, Marci.

Marci owns several restaurants, even when she's not working, she's still hosting people in some form. I had always wondered what it would be like to know Marci as a friend and not as her baby sister. People love her, respect her, and her employees will do anything for her. I feel like the two—make that three—meals we had with Sonia taking care of us, gave me an idea of exactly what Marci is like. A hint stern, but full of love, with a heart that thrives on giving—you'd also want her on your side if you're ever in a fight or in any type of trouble. It was lovely to have that impossible wish fulfilled.

Sonia said she likes to start the day with reggae or just listening to the birds, which she said were especially cheerful on this particular morning.

Matisyahu is now playing overhead. Peter said he is from Israel, which is the country we are going to next. The song that was playing was recorded in Austin, Texas. It's called "King Without a Crown." Peter and I listened to it a lot when we were beginning our relationship, but I'd never paid attention to the lyrics because the rap is so fast. Or maybe I just wasn't ready to truly hear them until now. The song starts with, "You're all that I have and you're all that I need. Each and every day I pray to get to know you please."

My memories of this song take me back to when Peter and I started dating. He was living in an apartment in south Tulsa. My girlfriend Sheila nicknamed it 81st and isle. It was on 81st Street and felt like an island. Peter grew up in the Florida Keys and he seems to bring that feeling to wherever he is.

Windows are usually open, colors are light with hints of corral, seafoam green and various shades of blue. Reggae is often playing in the background, and at the time, festive cocktails or his perfect margarita were never far away if someone wanted to celebrate the weekend at any time or day of the week. The apartment was a happy place to be.

Peter and I first met after being set up on a blind date. Neither of us wanted to go, so our common friend didn't tell us that he was picking us both up to go to an art festival in downtown Tulsa. A Bud Light or two later, we became, and still are, great friends.

After Thanksgiving with his family in the Keys in 2008, we went scuba diving together by a reef not far from his mom's home. While we were underwater, he tried to hand me a shell covered with moss. I refused to touch it because I imagined a sea creature living inside it. He flipped it over and there was a ring glued inside. I stared at him underwater in confusion. He had a dive slate where he scribbled, "marry me?" I nodded, even though I still didn't fully comprehend that he had just proposed marriage to me underwater. When we came to the surface, the other scuba divers on the boat cheered and bottles of champagne were opened. Peter later explained how he snuck coolers of bubbly onto the boat without me seeing anything. The only thing I noticed was that he was sweating a lot. I figured he was nervous about diving.

That night, his family and their closest friends took us out to celebrate by eating stone crabs—a cherished meal in the Keys. I remember his younger brother, Brett, sharing why the wedding ring is worn on the fourth finger. The tradition is ancient and began as a belief that the vein in the ring finger on the left hand ran directly to one's heart. Peter had my heart and his beautiful ring was now on my finger.

Our love is what sparked my love for God. Because before Peter, I was curious, but I wasn't actively seeking faith. To be honest, it made me uncomfortable. Once, after conducting an interview for our morning show *Good Day Tulsa*, a guest was leaving and said, "God bless you." I just stared at her. I later asked my co-anchor, Keith Taylor, "What do I say back?" It was like someone told me they loved me, but I wasn't quite ready to commit and respond with the same phrase. I think his response was, "just say thank you."

Peter got me a book called *The Shack*, written by William Paul Young. I resisted reading it. I'm sure it was not a coincidence that the author later became a guest on *Good Day Tulsa*, so I literally had to read the book if I wanted to be a decent interviewer.

The book broadened my perception of God. Before that, I saw God as distant, separate, possibly a punisher or one who casts judgement. Now, I see and experience God as love, oneness, closer than close, forgiveness and understanding. It's been more than ten years since that book helped launch my faith walk.

Around that same time, Yvonne was the weekend news anchor while I was working an opposite shift for *Good Day Tulsa*. Before we were friends through faith, she scared me. One day she walked up to me and said, "God is fighting for your soul." I remind her of that moment every now and then, but she doesn't remember it. That moment is carved into my memory because it was so shocking. First off, Yvonne spoke to me, which was a big deal for me. Second, she said, "God is fighting for your soul."

I had to do a morning news cut-in with Keith directly after that and I remember asking him, "What do you think that means?" He put up with a lot from me. I was so young and inexperienced at life—and there I was—his co-anchor. I remember asking him a question that got the response, "just be yourself," but I had no idea how to do that yet, "just be myself?" I was so young.

So, movement was happening in our efforts to find God. Before that movement started happening, this question kept coming to mind, "is this it?" Meaning, "Is this all there is to life?"

Peter and I started shopping for a church for guidance. Each Sunday we'd try a different one. I felt like Goldilocks and the Three Bears. One church literally didn't fit—Peter's legs were too long to fit in the pews. The last one we tried was one of the larger churches in town. The sermon that day discussed couples who live together before marriage are sinners. Peter and I were living together during our engagement. We didn't feel like sinners, or like we were going to hell.

Driving home after hearing that sermon, I can still see us in the car together in the rain. I remember saying with a firm belief, "there has to be something else." And there was.

I was watching a lot of *Oprah* and while reading a book in her book club, there was a requirement to learn how to meditate before continuing on in the book, but how do I learn to meditate? Within a week or so, I was taking a Bikram Yoga class taught by our friend Teresa. As she was wrapping up the class, she said she needed to leave quickly because she was hosting a meditation at her home that night. That's it! She knows how I can learn! She suggested we learn the basics from a local nun who had been teaching meditation for decades. During the nun's class, we learned breathing techniques and focused our eyes on a candle—it was all very calming and a great first step. The meditation fire had been lit.

After another Bikram Yoga class, Peter noticed a light blue book in the corner of Teresa's studio. It was the *Autobiography of a Yogi* by Paramahansa Yogananda.

After Peter read it, he pushed me to follow suit and read it. When I got to the chapter about Kriya Yoga meditation, everything in me said, "yes, yes, yes," and "is this real?"

I couldn't get back to yoga class fast enough to ask Teresa about it. She confirmed Kriya yoga meditation is real and she has practiced it for decades.

In general, the technique helps you slow your breath, focus your mind, and gradually lose awareness of the body so you can feel God's presence in the form of Divine peace.

I knew it would be the way for me to finally experience God, and I was right.

# Mark

## *Day 46*

## *Santiago de Compostela, Galicia, Spain*

We barely made it to our bus this morning from "the end of the world" Finisterre to get back to Santiago. We fly out tomorrow, but came back early today for brunch. Sounds odd, but this would be our fourth and final Camino brunch with our Australian friend Mark.

We met Mark on the first day of walking the Camino. There's something really special about the people you meet on your first day. It feels like a pledge class of a fraternity. But the only hazing involved would include café con leches and walking a lot of steps.

We met Mark right after Laura, and actually, we met him because of her. When Laura sat down to talk to us near the apple tree on that first day, what she shared with us was so fascinating I thought, "this would be a great podcast episode," but by the time I realized I should ask to formally interview her, it was too late—it was time to start walking again. So, as I walked away, I thought, "the next person I meet, I'm going to ask to do a podcast interview."

I don't necessarily want to do them—and asking people for an interview is literally the most difficult part for me. But as I was preparing for the Camino, I can't tell you how many people said, "you should do a podcast." Over and over it kept coming to us. The most distinct time was when I went to a coworker in another department at NBC-5 to ask about pitching a travel-television series. His response? "You should do a podcast." Okay fine, I'll try to figure out how to do a podcast. Another co-worker offered unsolicited advice about audio-recording gear and I was off and running. I just needed that first person to interview.

My reporter senses were on high alert after leaving Laura. As I walked, I waited for the next person to come into our Camino experience. We checked into the only albergue in Orisson, which is the halfway point between Saint-Jean-Pied-de-Port, France and Roncesvalles, Spain.

I was just about finished getting my bunk bed settled in the pilgrims' dorm, when Crocodile Dundee walked in—same accent, similar hat and disheveled hair. I loved that movie and watched it countless times as a kid.

Within a few minutes, we were having a spiritually-focused conversation and I knew he was perfect for our attempt at a podcast. Fortunately, he was happy to oblige.

I asked him if it was hard leaving things behind in order to do the Camino. He answered by explaining that he'd been "leaving" his whole life. He was a sailor for 20 years and always found joy in his next adventure.

I got a hint at what I was later going to learn from Mark when I asked him if finishing the Camino was his goal. He said he had no expectations of finishing. That threw me, because usually my goal when starting anything is to finish. It's the ending that I look forward to because that's the accomplishment. In this case, and with this friendship with Mark during our six-weeks on the Camino, sprinkled with a few brunches and walking together a few times and talking, my perspective of finishing the Camino was changed. It took a bit, but I finally realized the lesson I needed to learn from Mark was, "not having expectations."

He said he didn't expect to finish the Camino because he wanted to give himself the opportunity to quit at any time and for any reason. No expectations meant no false-sense of failure.

Mark did finish his Camino. As the three of us spent time together in Santiago, we talked in depth about the topic of reaching the end. Mark explained that for him, the Camino wasn't about finishing and getting his Compostela certificate to prove he walked the last 100 kilometers—it was about the experience. It was about all the parts in the middle. He said the people are what made his Camino special. It's not the destination—it's the experience.

I took that as an analysis for life. On the various Caminos, pilgrims are all heading to the same place: Santiago. In life, we are all heading to the end of life. It's going to happen to all of us, but for whatever reason, many of us (including me) rarely think about the shared commonality of death. So, what if my focus on life was more about "the experience," not accomplishments or money. "God loves me and wants me to be happy," is the clear message I'd received from my out-of-body experience with psilocybin mushrooms. Mark clarified that there is a line between being carefree and being careless. We still need money, but I need to do a better job at not letting money control my decisions. I should choose the experience of life.

The "expectations bug" bit me in a bad way early on, and it taught me an important lesson—that expectations are all in my head and I am the only one who creates my own suffering when those expectations aren't met.

One of the few towns I fully researched before coming to the Camino was Larrasoaña. I thought the name was beautiful, so I hyper-focused on it for whatever reason. I imagined walking into town, I'd meditate inside its historic church, then I'd eat a specific food at the outdoor seating area of the café nearby. It was all done in my head weeks before arriving.

So, when we finally walked into town, we were more than ready for a break (needing food, water, and time off our feet). But we walked in during siesta. The whole town was shut down and would be for the next three hours. The church was closed too. I was so disappointed and a bit frustrated with the situation. But why? I was only frustrated because my expectation of a future event didn't happen as I'd planned it in my mind. That's ridiculous, because it's impossible to control something you don't have control over.

I'd basically set myself up to fail. On the contrary, I could still do the same research, but if I don't have an expectation that it will be a certain way—it's a neutral experience and a great joy if anything comes of it.

The Camino taught that lesson to me over and over again in the form of coming into small towns. Will there be anything to eat, drink, or see? Will it be open? Who knows, but slowly my expectations were released, and I was able to just appreciate anything a town had to offer.

It's such a subtle way to learn a lesson, but when it comes up several times a day for six weeks, the lesson can grow within you at a deeper level, then later be applied to other things in life.

I got word yesterday that a freelance opportunity I had planned for after we get back home is not going to work out. That test is a bit bigger than the one felt in Larrasoaña, but it's the same test. I expected to do a job and reap the benefits of its paycheck, but it didn't happen and there's nothing I can do about it. I didn't fail because I was replaced by someone more qualified—it just didn't happen. Maybe I'm going to need that time to do something better, or nothing at all and I'll be resting. I'm neutral. I'm being shown in countless small ways that if something doesn't work out, it's because it'll work out better for me later.

Being disappointed is a horrible feeling that is all in my head—so why punish myself? Plan and prepare, but be open to the outcome with limited expectations of the results—especially if there are elements that are out of my control—that's what I learned from Mark. He's a super-happy dude who types g'day in emails. Having no expectations seems to be treating him well. I need to be more like Mark.

# Kristin P.

## Day 47

## Santiago de Compostela, Galicia, Spain

We beat the Santiago airport employees to the airport today. Compared to yesterday, when we woke up in Finisterre at 9 a.m. and needed to catch a bus to Santiago at 9:20 a.m. This morning we actually woke up on time and made it promptly to meet our scheduled taxi outside our hotel at 3:35 a.m.

On the way here, Peter pointed out that the best parts of our Camino were the unexpected experiences that took place just off the main Camino.

After we enjoyed brunch with Mark for the first time on my birthday—following our pre-sunrise hike to Alto del Perdón to shoot the Monument to the Pilgrim sculpture as the sun rose—we met Kristin P.

We were getting close to the turnoff to a 12$^{th}$ century church, built in the shape of an octagon. It is the Iglesia de Santa Maria de Eunate and it's surrounded by fields of sunflowers (instead of a town, like most other churches).

The church was a few kilometers of extra walking for the day. We wanted to do it, but were hesitant to add the extra distance. Near the turnoff, Kristin P. was standing there. She, too, was in the same mindset and we decided to walk to see the church together, getting to know each other along the way. It was worth every step.

Afterward, we sat on the grass in the shade near the church and shared a picnic of olives, sausage, fruit, and a cheese sandwich that Kristin P. contributed. She shared that she transitioned from a life in the corporate world to one dedicated to spirituality. She suggested that to help me transition, I write down a list of words or titles that I no longer want to be associated with—then burn that list. I still need to make that list.

It's now time to board our flight out of Santiago. The next stop on our pilgrimage is Israel, where we'll spend the next ten days.

KRISTIN DICKERSON

# Israel

# Camping In Israel

## Day 49

## She'ar Yashuv, Israel

Love bubble. Yes, of course, I was about to eat something delicious. We were sitting at a picnic table in a community camping area in a kibbutz in She'ar Yashuv. It's in the north of Israel near the border of Lebanon and Syria.

Our host in Israel is Rosemary. Her adult daughter invited us to camp with her family and a friend starting tonight and lasting into late tomorrow afternoon. The campgrounds consist of about a dozen families, many of which have young children.

All the food is cooked over fires at a designated area near the entrance of the campground. Each group that is camping seems to have its own metal pot that's filled with various goodies like vegetables and rice (or meat for those who eat it, but our group is mostly vegan).

After we walked in, a man in a golf cart dropped off sleeping pads for me and Peter.

It's Yom Kippur. A day dedicated to atonement for the Jewish people. The people at this campsite are not Jewish, or if they are, they are not actively practicing their faith according to tradition.

From what I understand, the entire country shuts down for this religious day starting around sunset and ending around sunset the following day. That time is spent fasting (not even drinking water), in prayer, and asking God to forgive sins. Shops close. No one drives. We tried to buy fuel several hours before the shutdown started, but even a pay-at-the pump option was no longer an option. The roads are empty of cars and replaced with kids on bicycles. It's taken very seriously.

We asked the non-Jewish people we are with a series of questions about how and why the country comes to a halt.

"What happens if you drive anyway?" I asked.

"Well, we don't."

"But why?"

"Because we respect the beliefs of our neighbors."

How incredible that commerce in an entire country can shut down in respect of religious beliefs, and even more impressive to me, is the people who do not follow that religion also respect it. Our group respects it, but chose to leave the cities to avoid the limitations.

After dinner was eaten at the respective campsites, children and their parents gathered around a half circle to watch a fire dancer. The young lady twirling a blazing baton didn't take payment or tips because she was there with friends.

Yesterday, Peter and I went with Rosemary to a grocery store to buy food for this trip. While waiting near a checkout lane, a man asked us why we were in Israel. Peter said it was to visit Holy sites. The man said, "this whole country is Holy. So many Holy men have walked here." He went on to tell us about a few places where our "friend Jesus" used to visit, which includes the north of Israel near our campgrounds.

Peter and I have enjoyed camping throughout our relationship, but for one reason or another we've never slept under the stars without a tent. Usually it's because of the weather—either too cold or we were concerned the morning dew would get us wet.

Since this camping trip was a last-minute invitation, our only choice was to sleep without a tent and fortunately we had a perfectly clear view of the sky.

We laid down on our borrowed sleeping pads and wrapped our bodies in our bedding from the Camino. Our eyes were wide open with hopes of seeing a shooting star. About 15 minutes later, we saw one. It was a glorious sight.

I felt the need to verbally remind us about the uniqueness of the situation. "Peter, we're in Israel, camping, watching the stars in a place where Jesus once was. This is nuts."

Peter reminded me to check my phone in case I got an update from my family. My father had a mild stroke the day before and was in the hospital in Tucson, Arizona. A text from my mom said he was speaking and appeared fine, but they were running tests to figure out what caused the stroke.

I also received a text from my former general manager. He asked if I was interested in a position anchoring a half-hour show that was upbeat and positive. It's not news, instead, there would be sponsored segments, live interviews and feature stories. I'd also have a stronger role in choosing the stories that would be broadcast.

Now isn't this a confusing predicament. Isn't this exactly what I wanted? To share positive stories with the world? Or would it be taking a step backward? Just two days ago, we were talking about moving to Ecuador or doing a hike through Japan to visit 88 temples in 90 days. Or there's the option of buying an RV to travel the US and shoot stories for fun.

If we stayed mobile, we'd likely not try to have children. If we take this new offer, we'd have a dependable income and that security would likely influence us to try and conceive. Instead of a fork in the road, this feels like a capital T for Two very different directions.

The next day, the sun was shining, and we all walked to a nearby river to take a dip in the cold water from the mountains. I dipped three times. I later learned that our swimming hole is one of three tributaries that feed into the Jordan River—where Jesus was baptized—and flows into the Sea of Galilee—where Jesus walked on water.

When we got back to our campsite, a neighbor boy asked if any of us had paper he could use to draw. I'd left my two journals at Rosemary's home, so the boy was out of luck.

Everyone laid down to rest and I checked my phone again for any updates on my dad. Nothing new from my family, but I got an email from a friend and former co-worker named Brad. He is a beautiful writer and he asked if I was writing a book about our experience on the Camino.

I thought of the text from the night before from my former GM asking if I was interested in coming back to work. If I agreed, I'd be asked to sign a new talent contract that gives the company full rights to my image and anything I create, which potentially, could include a book.

Just as I thought that, Peter woke up from his nap and mumbled, "talent release, it's in your vest pocket, give it to the kid." I had kept two copies of a generic talent release in my pocket in case I interviewed someone who I might put in our Camino documentary. It's basically a shorter version of the one I'd sign with the TV station if I went back to work.

So just like that, I gave away two talent release contracts to a kid to use as scratch paper for drawing. Significant? Or coincidence? If significant, is giving away two contracts a sign that I don't need to sign one? Scratch paper can be seen as trash, or as rebirth because it's found a second life—a second purpose that's way more fun, creative and beautiful.

Is this a test? I feel like the answer to this conundrum is going to be made very clear, but how soon? At some point, I'll need to respond to my former GM's text asking if I'm interested in hosting the new show.

It's now midday and I'm sitting at our campsite. I just looked up and saw a large flock of birds flying. Earlier, our swimming group noticed a similar sight. I mentally noted that I didn't see them flap their wings. They just soared so effortlessly. I said, "I need to be more like them, less flapping," meaning I need to let the wind carry me and try to reduce unnecessary struggle in my life. The birds choose when they need to use their energy, where to put their effort.

Now when I saw them an answer came, "I can't solve a problem from the same plane it was created on," which is a paraphrase of someone else's paraphrase of an Albert Einstein quote.

When it comes to a decision about returning to work in Texas—I need a broader perspective.

# Spiritual Battle

## Day 52

## Tirat Carmel, Israel

I'm just going to put this all out there with no filter. I don't know yet if it's significant. I just had a dream that ended with me screaming to the sky (while dreaming), declaring "I'm waking up now! I'm waking up now!" But the demon just kept attacking me.

The demon looked like a three-way combination of the evil being in *Harry Potter*, a mask from the movie *Scream*, and a male cyclist (he was wearing cycling shorts). At one point, I was fighting it off and its black cape became empty. I'd won. But then the white body within it reappeared.

Before I go any further, I need to note that God preceded the demon—in the dream, and in our activities earlier on in the day.

Today we visited a holy site for the Bahá'í faith in Haifa, Israel. Then we went looking for Elijah's Cave. Conveniently, we found it on Google Maps. We arrived at the Basilica of our Lady of Mount Carmel, which is located inside the Monastery of Stella Maris. As we walked inside, we saw the rock-walled cave underneath the church. A pamphlet at the door stated, "In the lower part of the presbytery we find the ancient cave often inhabited by Elijah the great leader and father of the prophets." We meditated near his cave and did our best to feel God and Elijah's presence.

In the first part of my dream, I was with a group of people in a two-story log cabin. I was resting on a cot in the upper room when I fell asleep—making this a dream within a dream.

I saw myself in the mountains like the ones we saw near the Sea of Galilee on the way to our campsite. It was at night. I looked down and saw a bear cub. I thought, "danger!" because momma bear must be close. That's when God's giant hands scooped me up and raised me a hundred or so feet above the bear cub. I could feel my feet dangling like I was on a swing-ride at a county fair—there was a little resistance, but my legs could still swing freely. God's hands gently set me down on the next hilltop.

The second part was waking from that dream (while still dreaming) and I sat up on my cot. I saw golden leaves blow under a soft white spotlight and I thought, "that is God." Then a gentle breeze swept through the room moving the sheer white curtains on the windows. I thought, "that is God."

Then there was a major shift. In my dream, I tried to tell my sister Kari about my God dream, but she was drunk and completely out of it. I saw my mom outside the cabin, near a field, and she was distracted—maybe looking at a horse. Then I saw them—two horses were woven into barbed wire. They were dead.

When I woke up and remembered seeing the horses, I wept. I thought about how significant horses had been on our Camino—helping us climb a mountain or simply walking to a fence near us for a scratch.

In the La Rioja region of Spain, two horses with riders surprised us as they came trotting down a dirt road through fields of olive trees and grapevines. They seemed like a vision from heaven.

Then, after our group went swimming in North Israel, we were walking back to our campsite when three horses seemed to, once again, appear out of nowhere. They crossed a stream, walked right in front of us and stopped, then two of them fell asleep while standing there.

In my dream, the two horses were dead. Eyes closed, wire holding their disfigured bodies in a way that could not have been done by humans.

Back upstairs in the cabin (still dreaming), my new Sony camera was sitting in mud, the lens was covered with red clay. I saw Peter. He was out of his mind, too. He was holding my first Sony camera (that I used when I was learning to shoot) and he threw it on the ground—cables and all, right into the mud, ruining it. "Why would he do that?" I thought.

Then came the demon. His cot was near mine. He started grabbing at my feet like he was trying to get me in a sexual manner. It just kept getting worse. I fought so hard trying to get him away. As he came after me, his image became more tormented.

I finally screamed, "I am waking up now!" But I didn't. I was still stuck inside that log cabin with a black-caped demon who couldn't be killed. Before finally waking up, I was desperately searching for a scripture of protection, but I couldn't remember one in my dream.

Thoughts upon waking: I need to prepare for spiritual battle—possibly in Jerusalem. Instead of meeting that demon on its own level—with violence, anger and hate, I can only beat evil with love, peace and God's protection. I need a scripture. A simple one to use as a mantra the next two days before we arrive in the Old City.

I also thought of the distractions I've had since arriving in Israel. My dad had a health scare, and this new job opportunity. Are they both legit—or distractions? The timing is now suspicious to me. I've spent two days thinking about the potential job. Two days wasted on a future possibility that can be pondered far after I've left the holiest land in the world.

In my dream, all of my securities and comforts were taken. The people who all pour love into me—Peter, Kari and my mom—had simply lost their minds. The cameras were damaged. The horses were dead.

That demon was so freaking scary.

Not having control in the dream world is scary. So, the only place I can beat the demon is in my conscious state.

I'm convinced that our placement with Rosemary for a week before visiting Jerusalem is not a coincidence. We eat vegan food, have group meditations and do yoga. We couldn't be in a better place to prepare for spiritual battle.

This also came to mind while processing this dream: I need to be prepared to be a prayer warrior at any moment. Being over-caffeinated (or caffeinated at all) changes my inner-heart vibration and keeps me from being fully able to serve and respond to God's call. It's going to be hard, but I need to give up coffee.

# Leaving The North Of Israel

## *Day 53*

## *Tirat Carmel, Israel*

We're on a bus heading to Jerusalem. We spent one week with Rosemary in the North of Israel. She not only treated us like guests, she treated us like guests of God. Each meal was made from scratch and vegan. She made her own almond milk every few days that she added to our nightly chai and morning coffee. One of my favorite food surprises was her mango chutney that was spiced with tiny peppers from her garden that is grown on the windowsill of her second-story condo in the town of Tirat Carmel.

Her bread was made by hand while we watched and there was never an expectation for us to lift a finger, in fact she simply wouldn't allow it. What a wonderful way to start our journey in Israel.

Rosemary is a recently-retired midwife. She is also a yoga instructor and student of all things holistic. We have a running list in our minds of all the ways we are going to live more like Rosemary. She taught us a yoga practice that can be done at home, inspired us to make vegetarian food and bread from scratch, and impressed us with her efforts to care for the environment by picking up other people's trash while creating little of her own.

While being spoiled, I was also feeling a bit guilty. Not because Rosemary waited on us hand and foot—I just enjoyed that part—but I felt guilty that I haven't been working enough toward my initial goal of sharing stories about faith. I set those expectations before I decided to stop setting expectations. So, the damage had already been done and now it seems impossible to remove them.

The expectations I set included posting an edited video about faith once a week while walking the Camino.

Those expectations were made long before I felt the weight of a 30-pound pack, before I realized how tired I'd be after walking 10 miles and shooting video during rest stops, and before I realized that the hours spent inside editing video were hours not spent outside enjoying the people at our albergues. So, my expectations were not met. Does that mean I've failed? We're roughly halfway through this three-month pilgrimage, is it already a failure?

I was thinking about these things as we went for a walk today up a mountain behind Rosemary's condo. This is the first time we've walked more than two miles in nature since we first arrived in Santiago two weeks before. I can't express how helpful it is to walk in nature. As I made each step up the rocky trail toward a series of caves near the top of the mountain, things in my mind started to piece together.

I realized that interviewing Rosemary would help us start one of our initial expectations—sharing stories that build faith. Over the last six days, we sat at her kitchen table and chatted with her as she made us countless meals, snacks and hot drinks. We were enjoying her chai with fresh almond milk when she shared the following story, which we asked her to re-tell in front of our camera an hour or so before we left her home and started heading toward Jerusalem.

*"My name is Rosemary. I live and work in Israel. I've been a devotee of Guruji [Paramahansa Yogananda] for 22 years and he's part of my daily life.*

*I do home and hospital deliveries. I'm a midwife. I had a patient that should've had a hospital delivery because the fetus was very large. She called me at about two in the morning and I went and examined her and realized that we would have to leave quite soon for the hospital.*

*I asked her where the babysitter was because there was a sibling, a 2-year-old. She said, "Oh, I'll call my mother," and after a while I said, "Where is your mother coming from?" She said, "Tel-Aviv," which is like an hour from Haifa. I realized that the child would be delivered at home.*

*The husband was really frantic and no help at all. Anyway, the baby's head was delivered, and the shoulders got stuck in the mother's pelvis, which is an expected complication of very large fetuses.*

*I just cried out in my soul, "Guruji, you have to help and help now!" And these instructions came in my mind. He told me to get her up on all fours and as she got up on all fours, the child slipped out.*

*I knew that Guruji delivered that child. In fact, I've always said when I deliver now, I always ask for his help. And I say, "You're the best midwife I know."*

# Jesus And Jerusalem

## *Day 54*

### *Jerusalem, Israel*

Song lyrics stuck in my head: "Jesus loves me, oh yes he does."

I struggled with my first experience in the Old City in Jerusalem. I struggled hard. It included an apology to Jesus. "Jesus, I love you and all, but I am struggling right now."

We booked tickets for a group tour so we could join Yvonne and her friend Carolyn. It included a quick stop at Mount of Olives, the room of the Last Supper and other notable locations that are significant to Jesus's life.

I knew there were going to be crowds, but I really had no idea how big they'd be. In Bethlehem, we waited in line for about an hour to see the site of Jesus's birth. Each group's tour guide was shouting at us to squeeze closer to the person in front of us in line. It was packed. My least favorite moment was kneeling down to touch the site of Jesus's birth and hearing someone close to me yell, "no pictures!" I was about to take a picture. I later learned if people take pictures it slows down the line and the tour guides don't like it because they are on a tight schedule.

Once removed from the day's intensity, I gained an appreciation for the many people traveling from around the globe to get closer to "my friend Jesus" and also the hired tour guides who make it possible to see a dozen or so historical sites in the course of seven hours. I think that was my problem, I was doing a lot of seeing, but absolutely no feeling. My spiritual spidey-senses were registering absolutely nothing. I was dry as could be.

At the end of our tour in Bethlehem, we were dropped off at a store. As soon as I walked in, I knew it—we were "exiting through the gift shop." I realize people need to make a living, but I just wasn't in a place to help a pushy sales person make a profit on religion.

After telling several store employees I wasn't going to buy anything, I saw it.

It was a carved wooden statue of Jesus washing the feet of a disciple. I immediately saw Rosemary's image in the carving of Jesus, and Peter and me as the person getting cared for. I realized we had been experiencing Jesus's love for the past week through Rosemary.

It was in Jesus's birthplace that I once again realized how God works through people.

After the tour dropped us off at Yvonne's hotel in Jerusalem, Peter and I went to run an errand. We quickly realized that the beginning of another Jewish holiday had shut down shops and restaurants. So, we kept strolling and went through Jaffa Gate where we were grateful to find restaurants and vendors still selling items to tourists. We drank fresh pomegranate juice, followed by a slice of pizza and a cup of coffee (I'm drinking less coffee, but haven't fully given it up yet). We then wandered back into the Christian Quarter.

I felt the need for a redo of the day—and I got one.

The sun was starting to set, the weather was cool, and the crowded walkways were now quiet and relatively empty. I couldn't seem to walk slow enough, actively feeling the ground beneath my feet. It felt so nice. There was no yelling, no bumping, no tour guide snapping at me saying "hey girl, move forward." What a delightful place to be. Peter gently suggested I walk a little faster and we eventually wandered back to the Church of the Holy Sepulchre—the site of Jesus's crucifixion, burial and resurrection.

We didn't see any tour groups, like earlier on in the day. During this second visit, I was able to take as much time as I wanted to lay my head and hands on the stone where Jesus' body was prepared for burial.

We listened to a group of young men, dressed in black robes, sing while they walked around the Edicule, which is a structure within the church that preserves the location of Jesus's tomb.

We walked around to a side hallway then down a set of stairs. It was amazing. It felt like we were in a cave, surrounded by rock walls and a soft golden light shining upon them. There were moments of up to five minutes when Peter and I were the only ones there. We sat down on a step and did our best to feel the peace offered within the room.

Peter would agree that I rarely sing, but when I do it's for God, and God alone. On the Camino, when I'd find myself in an empty church or a tunnel with great acoustics, only one thing came to my mind and it had to be sung aloud for God. "Oh, thou King of the infinite, I behold thee in samadhi." Samadhi is a Sanskrit word that means union with the Divine. While sitting on that step in the Church of the Holy Sepulchre, we sang that song to God once again, "Oh thou King of the infinite, I behold thee in samadhi."

Our evening experience in the Church of the Holy Sepulchre was the most peaceful re-do I could have ever imagined. It served as a reminder that if something isn't the experience you hoped for—do it again, and do it better.

# Meeting Yvonne In Israel

## *Day 55*

### *Jerusalem, Israel*

Dear Divine Intervention, thank you.

On our second day in Jerusalem, there was a mix-up with our scheduled group tour. The driver gave a handler an incorrect time, and we didn't get picked up for the tour.

One lesson that is now ingrained in me from walking the Camino de Santiago is that when something doesn't work out, it's because it is going to work out better later. Knowing this, I was thrilled about the unexpected adventure that was about to unfold before us.

Our party of four was now on its own. Within an hour, we were in a brand-new white Mercedes van driving us on a private trip to Nazareth, the Sea of Galilee (specifically, the site where Jesus fed 5,000 people with two fish and five loaves of bread), and the Jordan River where John the Baptist baptized Jesus. Adventure!

Our two travel companions, Yvonne and Carolyn, are both experts on scripture and all-things spiritual, so any history lesson we needed was just a whisper away.

The fact that we are all here together is a miracle in itself. By chance, Yvonne "just happened" to schedule this trip to Jerusalem at the exact same time as us—and none of us knew it until the flights were booked.

When I got my first reporting job working weekends at Tulsa's Channel 8, and Yvonne was the anchor, I had no idea what I was doing as a novice reporter. I was (and still am) in awe of Yvonne's knowledge, beauty, self-awareness and strength of faith.

She left a 27-year career in TV-news in order to dedicate her life to serving God, and for these two days, she was our travel companion as we visited holy sites throughout Israel.

Thank you, Divine scheduler, for making our trip to Israel better than we could have ever imagined, or planned for ourselves.

KRISTIN DICKERSON

# India

# The Shift

## *Day 59*

## *Noida, Uttar Pradesh, India*

I've got a hellacious dark cloud over me. It started before meditation. We took a car from the hotel to the ashram and I wasn't ready for the close encounters with volunteers. One was in my face asking me three times if my cell phone was off. Then pointing to exactly where I need to put my shoes. Then several other lady volunteers showed me exactly where I needed to sit, by winding me through different aisles of empty seats–all to sit with our eyes closed for meditation. I'm going to stop listening to their directions. Like an older Indian woman, I'll do what I want.

What am I doing here?

We're at a meditation retreat that's being conducted mostly in Hindi. My feet are eaten up with mosquitos in the exact locations where I didn't put bug repellent this morning. Meditation felt like torture. Prayer in Hindi, brief chant, silence and stillness for an hour. What a long hour.

What am I doing here?

There are several classes in English, which are the same classes I've attended for the last ten years on this path. What are the chances I'll learn something new?

I'm tired of being stared at. I'm a white-ish woman in India attempting to blend in by wearing the Indian-style clothing that is required in the ashram. They still stare. Mostly Indian women. Up and down. Likely asking, "What is she doing here?" Peter, on the other hand, gets asked for a picture. Young, small Indian dudes just want to take a picture with him and his broad shoulders.

These things happen each time we come. Sometimes the shift in culture is easy—this time, not so much.

The hardest time was the first time. I arrived, but my luggage didn't. So, we got to the ashram for a silent retreat and I basically had nothing but the clothes on my back. Peter and I were married at the time, but I never changed my last name—so we couldn't stay together. I had no bedding, no clothes, no towel for a shower, nothing.

I found my bedroom, briefly met my female roommate and then left. When I returned, the door was locked, and I didn't have a key. I found my roommate and she told me she'd hid my key in a planter, which I never found. That created the hardest and longest dark cloud I had ever experienced at that time.

Everything I came to depend on had been stripped away. My life revolved around my job as a news anchor in Tulsa, a town that was big, but still small enough to usually be met with a smile wherever I went. That comfort was now gone. I was outside of my safe fishbowl and needed to start from scratch.

A few days after our arrival, my roommate left, so I had my bedroom to myself. I was alone. The top of the outside wall of the room was open to the street, so loud music blared into my room all night. It was unsettling to say the least. I slept with the lights on.

Inside the ashram, men and women eat separately, meditate separately, all separate. Peter and I had also read some false information before the trip. Peter was convinced we couldn't hold hands in public because affection was not allowed in India—false. He said I shouldn't look men in the eyes—also false. So, before I even arrived, I had some preconceived resistance. It was a long seven days.

While waiting for a courier to deliver my delayed luggage to the ashram, I purchased some cheap Indian clothing. I didn't have makeup or any products to make my hair look presentable—so I didn't feel like I looked good, and this was at a time in my life when my appearance was very important to me. There was also a lingering pressure from work that I needed to look perfect, but in India, I was far from it.

I don't remember what started my path out of the darkness. I think I texted Yvonne and said I was in trouble, but I'm not sure exactly.

Since I couldn't talk to Peter, and I was failing to make any new friends, I came to a realization. I needed to talk to God the same way I talk to Peter. In the past, if something exciting happened, I'd bubble with anticipation of sharing with Peter my thoughts about every aspect of the event. God needed to be that role. I needed to make God an active member of my life; not just during the troubling times when I needed His help, but all of the tiny insignificant moments that I might share with Peter. God needed to be "my person," and I needed to be the one to treat Him that way—so I did.

I started to walk through the ashram gardens pointing out the beautiful flowers and asking Him how He created something so unique and beautiful. As I walked, I'd recognize the muscles, joints and tendons in my body, then thank God for the ability to move forward with ease. I'd eat a meal in silence while having an inner conversation with God about which serving of food He liked best—was it the rice and dahl or the tortilla-like bread served with it. And how do they get the dahl so consistent? It's a perfect balance between soup and substance. When I changed my experience from "me" to "we," I started having a lovely time.

Then came my appearance. I decided I was going to try to feel beautiful from the inside and see if it was noticed on the outside. My luggage still hadn't arrived, and I had purchased a white, embroidered blouse that went down to my mid-thigh (a requirement of the ashram includes covering your bum with more than just britches—my words, not theirs).

I washed my hair with a bar of soap, attempted to make it curly, then put it in a loose ponytail. My skin was broken out, but as I looked at my bare face in the mirror, I tried to see a glow that resided deep within my soul. I looked hard and finally connected with the spark often seen in someone's eyes when they're filled with joy.

My efforts were noticed. The lady running the kitchen looked at me up and down and said, "You are looking very nice." Mission accomplished.

The dark cloud was nearly lifted completely. I was now enjoying my time alone with God while reaching the one-week mark inside the ashram.

There was a Kriya yoga ceremony where monks would be blessing new initiates who are seeking God-communion through the Kriya yoga technique of meditation.

I had heard this ceremony in India was different from the ones I had experienced in the US, when a monk gave individual blessings to the people dedicating their lives to experiencing God.

As the ceremony was about to start, I sat cross legged on the front row so I could see. To my eyes, nothing exceptional or out of the ordinary was happening, but to my heart, it was life changing.

I felt an abundance of love welling up inside me. As I write this now, my eyes are filling with tears and I can no longer see the lines on my journal's page.

I was experiencing a feeling of love unlike ever before.

Thoughts came about how beautiful it is to witness people dedicating their lives to seeking God. There's still no way for me to explain the source of the emotion other than I was experiencing God's love in full and it was overwhelming.

As soon as I got out of the ceremony, I speed-walked to the most sacred place on the ashram's grounds. I laid face down in front of the altar and cried. At that moment, I dedicated the rest of my life to God. I said in my mind and heart, "I'm yours. Do whatever you want with me." A tear just ran down my nose and once again the page lines are hard to see.

It was rare that I had that room to myself, but the ceremony had just ended so everyone else at the retreat was still busy receiving a blessed piece of fruit and rose petals from the monk leading the service.

In the room, I just laid there—forehead and nose still touching the floor, heart full of love and 100% committed to God. During that past week, everything I knew and depended on had been stripped away from me. I resisted releasing those things with all my might, but I finally broke.

I came away with a new understanding. All of the things that had been stripped away from me that week were the things I had been spending all of my time on: my ego and attachment to my job, my appearance, and my relationship with my husband. But the only thing that will go with me after I die—is God. He's the only thing I had coming into this world, and He'll be the only thing I have going out of it. So why wasn't I dedicating any time to Him? From then on, I promised to make God my priority.

# Challenges

## *Day 63*

## *Ranchi, Jharkhand, India*

We just arrived back at the same ashram in Ranchi where I dedicated my life to God. It feels amazing here. It's been raining, so the ground is moist, but not muddy. The grass is extra green and the flowers—well, I've never seen them bigger. One of the outdoor meditation areas is lined with violet dahlias. It's a flower I first fell in love with while nesting in our first home in Tulsa. Some varieties earned the term "dinner plate," because they can grow that big. They are outstanding. Countless thin petals of any color make up their abundant blooms. Some are round and soft, while others are sharp and even twisted.

I was admiring these flowers and trying to take their pictures, when a monk walked by and got our attention. As I was holding my camera, he asked Peter if he was a photographer. Peter said he was a drone pilot and takes aerial photographs and video. The monk said that wasn't necessary, he just needed him to take pictures at an upcoming speaking event at the ashram. Peter said that I was much better at taking photos, but the monk said I couldn't take the pictures because I'm a woman.

My blood started to boil just a bit.

Fortunately, we were interrupted by a more senior monk who has become a friend and life advisor over the years. The part of me that likes to ask questions, let them fly. I asked, "If there is one job and a female candidate is more qualified than a male candidate, why should the job be awarded to the male candidate?"

After pressing our monk-friend for 15 minutes about equality in India and the lack of equality in the ashram, I finally accepted an answer. He said, "If there are younger, male monks who need to work with the photographer who took these pictures, it would be easier and more acceptable for them to work with a man." Okay, I can understand that.

Two hours later, I was thinking about the topic of the "more qualified person" getting or keeping a job. There have been several times in my TV-news career, when I was not the more qualified person, but I got someone else's job. I never thought about it at the time, I just figured the older and more qualified woman just happened to retire and I just happened to be waiting in the wings—hungry for a promotion or a new challenge. I was not the more qualified candidate—she was. She had decades more experience, a sharper skillset and more knowledge of the towns and topics we were covering. I was younger, cheaper and less experienced.

So, am I currently the best candidate for this volunteer-photography job at the ashram? Now that my blood has stopped boiling, my mind is able to see that I might not be. I'm not sure I've worked hard enough to back up my passion.

I love taking pictures. I love that taking pictures forces me to constantly look for beauty. When I see that beauty, I stare at it to analyze what makes it beautiful.

I think the introvert in me also likes being behind a camera because it makes me feel like there's a protective barrier between me and the world around me.

I've invested a lot of money in having high-quality equipment for photography; however, I haven't necessarily dedicated the time to learn my camera beyond its automatic settings. So, if I was asked to volunteer as a photographer for this speaking event, the camera would do the exact same job for me as it would for Peter, who has only used it a few times.

When we were speaking with our senior-monk friend, one of the examples I didn't accept from him was that if I was an Indian woman, I would never have questioned the ashram's decision to not let a female serve as a photographer—because it's just the way it is. The argument that formed in my head was this: no one has ever questioned such a rule because there hasn't been a woman with a high enough ranking in the organization to question it. That frustrates my core. I'm curious if this small personal experience of inequality will help me fight for others' equality back home. Passion always grows after you experience something first-hand.

Our monk-friend said I shouldn't take a decision like this personally; I should take it as a decision of spirituality. Maybe God is preparing Peter because he, too, will need to be a qualified photographer. Maybe I need to focus on listening and taking notes during the speaking event (instead of taking pictures) because there is a key lesson I'm supposed to learn. Sometimes we don't know why certain choices are made or opportunities are rejected, but God knows, so I need to accept everything as a lesson.

There's a part of me that still wants to fight. Peter said I shouldn't let my ego get involved, but as of this writing, I'm feeling the "want" to fight, disagree, and state my case. I haven't always been able to speak up. Now I'm ready to.

# Become A Master

## Day 84

### Coimbatore, Tamil Nadu, India

I need to become a master of my camera gear. So, if there's ever a time I could offer photography as a service to God, there will be no question if I am the best candidate—male or female.

To prepare, I need to practice taking pictures of something difficult, something that's unpredictable, something small, something that moves quickly and whose lighting changes.

I need to practice taking pictures of birds.

After a few days of trying (and my bird pictures looking horrible), I was scrolling through Instagram and saw a picture of a Dallas Cowboy—his toes in the endzone, his body halfway to the ground in a perfect line, football safely in his arms. I thought, that's a bird! What a perfect picture of capturing an object in motion. It was beautiful.

I sent a private message to the photographer who captured that photo and asked if he gave photography lessons, because if he did, I'd like to sign up. He was incredibly kind and gave me some suggestions since he wasn't teaching a course. I told him I wanted to learn how to take pictures of birds in flight. He sent me a list of settings for my camera and an explanation of why those settings are the best. I tried his suggestions and it helped tremendously!

I later saw a picture of that photographer with a former-coworker and she said what an honor it was to meet a

Pulitzer Prize winner. Incredible, once again, God put the absolute best person in our path to help us. In this case, that path was Instagram and that photographer was Tom Fox from the Dallas Morning News.

Look out, birds!

# Sari Not Sorry

## *Day 68*

## *Ranchi, Jharkhand, India*

I wanted to get a new outfit for Diwali. The Hindu festival of lights is one of the most popular celebrations in India. We would be celebrating it at the Yogoda Satsanga Ashram in Ranchi, a town located in the state of Jharkhand.

Outside the ashram, people lit fireworks and lined buildings with colorful lights; while inside, hundreds of candles illuminated the ashram's holy places of prayer and meditation.

While the sun was still up, we heard about the significance of Diwali. It's a holiday that celebrates the victory of light over darkness, good over evil, and wisdom over ignorance.

The day before the celebrations, Peter and I went to two clothing stores near the ashram, but nothing stood out as worthy of buying for Diwali. After our unsuccessful shopping trip, we were invited to dinner at the Nundy family's home, which is across the street from the ashram. Almost every time we've come to India, we've been fortunate to bump into the Nundys at different meditation retreats. They've become lovely friends.

After we ate with them the night before Diwali, they gave me an unexpected gift that brought a deep sense of fulfillment: a maroon sari with gold thread embellishments and sparkly stones.

During our first trip to India, I was mesmerized by the beautiful saris. The ashrams require traditional clothing, so there were many that I could admire. I'd stand in line for food and stare at the sari in front of me. I remember assessing the mystery of the sari as I stood there, "The top bodice fits perfectly, but how on earth did she get in it? There's no visible zipper, no elastic, no buttons. It's a mystery and it's beautiful.

I'd later learn that the blouse is custom made from cloth cut from the end of the sari fabric. There are snaps or hooks on the chest that secure it, which are then covered by perfect folds of fabric draped across the front. It's really a brilliant creation. It also fits you at all times—even if your weight fluctuates. Again, it's brilliant.

At the Nundys, their daughter helped drape the maroon and gold sari fabric over my clothes so I could get an idea of what it will look like once the blouse is stitched and the folds are tucked.

I don't know if it's because I've basically worn the same two shirts and two pairs of pants for the last two months, but something deep within me was stirred while looking at my new sari in the mirror.

It felt like my heart was getting a hug; but not from the outside, from the inside. I sat down on their couch with an overwhelming feeling of gratitude for God's thoughtfulness.

I didn't even know this was a personal desire until I experienced it being fulfilled.

# Sweta

## *Day 70*

## *Bodh Gaya, Bihar, India*

After leaving Ranchi, we are traveling to two cities that are considered the Holiest to several religions. First is Bodh Gaya, where the Buddha sat underneath the bodhi tree and received enlightenment; second, is Varanasi, which is the oldest city in India, the abode of Lord Shiva, and the holiest place for Hindus to make a pilgrimage—often taking a dip in the Ganges River, or after death, being cremated on its banks.

Our traveling partner for these adventures is Sweta (sounds like Sch-way-tuh).

She's eight years younger than us, but we often call her Momma Sweta.

A few days into our adventures together, I asked her why her handbag was so big. She said it's because she's traveling with two kids (me and Peter). She has everything in that bag: napkins, water, snacks—both homemade and store bought.

Before we launched our travels together, her family invited us to their home for lunch. In two buildings that are nearly attached, most of the family (Sweta's parents, aunts, an uncle, a brother, grandmother, and one grandchild) all live together. As we started to hear about their lives, we learned that their multi-family home is full of high-achievers: family members include several teachers, engineers, an attorney and a PhD student (Sweta).

Sweta, her father, mother and sister-in-law made us 13 individual dishes for lunch that day—all from scratch.

# Prayer In Bodh Gaya

## *Day 72*

## *Bodh Gaya, Bihar, India*

Song stuck in my head: "Oh Jesus, Krishna I love you, and I love Buddha too."

We came "home" from traveling—long day, tough roads, dust, poverty—and found chai, cookies, conversation and a warm welcome by Kiran (sounds like Keer-un). Kiran is in charge of the Daijokyo Temple and Guest House in Bodh Gaya. He is also a Kriya yoga devotee, which is how we came to know him—other devotees in India who go on retreat in Bodh Gaya often stay with Kiran.

We are fortunate to stay with him for the next four days. He'll be cooking for us, organizing our spiritual sightseeing to places of significance for Buddha, all while showering us with love, funny stories, spiritual insight and great company.

He told us to go upstairs to our rooms for our evening meditation, clean up, then return downstairs for dinner at 9 p.m.

He said he got a message on WhatsApp to pray for California. People there were surrounded by wildfires. I haven't watched or followed the news for more than two months. I started to pray for protection, but then I felt torn. What if losing a house is what someone needs to advance spiritually? For example, I've met cancer patients who say they wouldn't change their experience because the disease was a blessing. It helped them see God working through people to help them. They became stronger than they ever knew they could be. They had a new appreciation for life.

Peter and I have been struggling to figure out a prayer for ourselves. There's a story about a man praying for a car. He asked God for something humble just to help him get around. God had already planned for him to get the fanciest car, but the man prayed for less—so he got less.

What do we pray for if we have no idea what is best for us regarding our path in life? Maybe our prayer for ourselves should be the same as our prayer for others, "May Thy will be done. Mold our lives according to Thy will."

I remember speaking with a monk in Encinitas, California. We'd met him when we were first joining the Kriya yoga path and always enjoyed bumping into him when we visited Encinitas on retreat over the years. Before we left for this faith walk adventure, he told us he prays for us every day. I was shocked that he even thought of us, nonetheless, spent time praying for us. I said, "really?" He said, "Yes, right after I pray for my family I pray for Kristin and Peter." My eyes formed extra liquid and I nearly had tears. Prayer is so powerful and what a gift it was to know someone was praying for us.

Kiran said he prays for everyone that he's ever known—in the order that they came into his life. He said it started as a way to practice strengthening his memory, now there are around 500 people in his daily prayers. He said we'll be added to the end of his list. What an honor.

# Buddha's Guidance

## *Day 73*

## *Bodh Gaya, Bihar, India*

While at lunch, between visiting Holy sites around Bodh Gaya, I was handed four books about the Buddha to glance through while we waited for our food to arrive.

I picked *The Buddha's Ancient Path*, by Ven. Piyadassi Thera.

I prayed quickly and randomly opened to page 193 where I read: "From me the world should receive happiness not sorrow . . . There is no duty higher than to promote the happiness of the world."-King Asoka — the Great of India, who later became known as Dhammasoka.

# Kiran

## *Day 74*
## *Bodh Gaya, Bihar, India*

When we were getting ready to leave Bodh Gaya, Sweta was writing a thank-you note to Kiran for taking such good care of us during our stay. I simply couldn't find any words to properly express my gratitude. I did, however, read someone else's kind words, written on a note that was saved in Kiran's scrapbook, that perfectly explained our time with Kiran.

*"Our dear Kiranji,*

*We have just reached back home here in Ranchi, but a sense of nostalgia is upon us, for you gave us in these three days love which is usually associated with mothers alone. Memories of the time spent at our home at Bodh Gaya in your loving care will keep tugging us to more trips there. The selflessness, tirelessness, eagerness, thoughtfulness with which you cared for us reminds us of our Gurudeva Sri Sri Paramahansa Yoganandaji's words, 'God comes to us as relatives to test our love for Him, but He comes to us as friends to give Himself to us.'*

*How we missed your cooking when we sat down to lunch after arriving here! We felt perfectly at home at Bodh Gaya. The cleanliness at Daijokyo is commendable; the floors were squeaky clean and the incense fragrance as one enters the drawing room has a unique, uplifting, warm feel. We felt as if you had extended both your arms in a welcome embrace throughout. You gave so much of your time, energy and resources to help make our stay comfortable. You are a wonderful host Kiranji. Someone has said, 'It is more fun to talk with someone who doesn't use long, difficult words, but rather short, easy words like 'what about lunch?'*

*In diving friendship."*

After we left Bodh Gaya, a thought of clarity came to me: Kiran is Buddha. Just like Jesus was loving us through Rosemary, Buddha was caring for us through Kiran.

# Devotees

## *Day 74*

## *Varanasi, Uttar Pradesh, India*

I got a Facebook message that said it looks like people are welcoming us with open arms as we travel. Is that the case? I responded, "yes," and that the people we've met are wonderful. That was this morning and I'm still thinking about that comment tonight. Yes, the people are wonderful, but it isn't random. They are all connected.

Like the quote in the thank-you note to Kiran, "God comes to us as relatives to test our love for Him, but He comes to us as friends to give Himself to us."

We have literally been handed off from one Divine friend to the next. Kiran walked us to the cab and gave specific instructions to the driver on how to take us to the airport to fly to Varanasi. He also packed us food to take with us (after feeding us two huge meals within two hours of each other).

As we approached Varanasi, Sweta was on the phone with a fellow Kriya yoga devotee named Vipin (sounds like Vih-pen). He and his wife live in Varanasi and helped Sweta book our hotel and arrange other travel plans. As our cab drove us from the airport into the bustling city late at night and in heavy traffic (cars, pedestrians, bicycles and rickshaws), Vipin met us on the side of the road on his motorbike. He then followed our taxi, but somehow beat us to our hotel. He worked with our driver to navigate parking, then he took Sweta's luggage and walked us a football-field's distance to the hotel, navigating a street that was shoulder-to-shoulder with festival-goers. If he hadn't met us and escorted us to our hotel, I'm not sure how we would have successfully navigated the trip.

Sweta is also a Divine friend who has made our travel possible and extremely enjoyable by hand-delivering us to each location.

In the months before our arrival to India, Peter and I were consumed with moving, finalizing work, preparing for the Camino and then walking it. So Sweta organized our entire trip to India, purchased flights with her credit card, booked us into ashrams, found and reserved hotel rooms. She did it all, on top of being a 29-year-old PhD student.

These sweet people are incredibly busy with their own lives, but they have paused everything to take care of us. Tonight, Vipin wouldn't take our reimbursement for the down payment on our hotel room in Varanasi. His reasoning: we're all family—God's family.

What a wonderful family.

# We're All Beggars

## Day 75

## Varanasi, Uttar Pradesh, India

I'm having an issue with beggars. As thoughts started to come just now on the topic, a fly started landing on my face. I just slapped my own face—and missed the fly.

India has beggars. Peter gives them money and they triple in both numbers and intensity. At one Holy site in the mountains where Buddha meditated, children, elderly and a few people with disabilities lined the street that tourists use to walk up to the cave. We were warned ahead of time not to donate to the people begging. We were told the elderly live in the nearby village and begging gives them something to do; the children are also taken care of and happen to be on holiday that day.

We saw a man our age sitting on the side of the street, holding a silver pan to collect offerings. He was blind. Peter tried to be sly and quickly put money in his pan hoping no one else saw the exchange.

Immediately after, a little girl who was maybe seven years old, gave the blind man's face a push, then she ran after us and harassed us as we walked down the hill away from the cave.

When we got to Varanasi, a heavy-set woman with a baby met us as we got out of our taxi. The baby was coughing. At times the woman would pull on Peter's arm and then make a cup shape with her hand to ask for money. I pushed him forward and put myself in-between him and the begging woman. I was so bothered.

But here's where my head's at: during our interview with Kiran he was talking about Kriya yoga and how Paramahansa Yogananda's teachings have transformed his life. Kiran said he used to fight for whatever he wanted, but now he gives a prayer and leaves it to God (while also working his tail off).

Kiran said everyone is a beggar. Rich people go into the temples and beg—often bartering with God saying, "You do this, and I will give you that." He said it works, but it's begging. Then those rich people walk out of the temple and the poor people beg them for money. We're all the same— we're all beggars. But he said he's done begging.

His spiritual path has released his desires.

On this faith walk, why do aggressive beggars bother me when I'm in a place where I might also need to beg? Since I left my job to make this pilgrimage, I currently don't have a predictable income.

Or maybe dealing with street beggars is an opportunity to practice being firm, but not bothered—an opportunity to use my voice and be strong.

# Sari Dreams Fulfilled, Again

## *Day 76*

## *Varanasi, Uttar Pradesh, India*

During our last night in Varanasi, Peter wanted me to buy myself a stole (like a shall, but thinner) because India's oldest city is also known for having the best fabrics—specifically, hand-woven Banarasi silk.

By the end of the night, the biggest, best, and most elite sari company's co-owners were presenting me and Sweta with free, handwoven-silk stoles. Mine was pink with gold-thread accents in the form of flowers. I immediately put it around my neck and the ends fell near my knees. It was beautiful. Only God could do something like this, because there is no way on earth I could have created or forced this opportunity to happen.

The wish began during our arrival in Varanasi. I saw a sari displayed at the airport and Sweta explained it was a really big deal to buy one in that city. On the way to the hotel, I saw a billboard for a store called Shanti Banaras. The billboard's image showed an exquisite sari that was draped in a way I'd never seen before. It was captured with bright and vibrant photography, mixing modern and ancient vibes in one photo. Breathtaking. I found the store on Instagram and clicked, "follow."

The next day, Vipin and his wife were taking us out to try Varanasi street food. They drove us right past the Shanti

Banaras store. At that exact moment, Vipin's wife asked us if we wanted to do any shopping while we were in their city.

Later that night, on a whim, I sent an email request to the store's PR team asking to shoot some video of their fabrics for a story that might be shown on our Youtube channel. Surprisingly, they replied to the email and said, "yes." I was shocked because we had no affiliation with any real media outlet. We were technically just Americans who took their cameras on vacation. But they said "yes," so we went with it.

We arrived at their super-fancy store and told them we'd be done shooting our video within 30 minutes; however, their generosity, hospitality, and their tour just seemed to keep going. Almost four hours later, we left with full hearts.

At one point, Sweta said, "Any Indian woman would be very jealous of us right now."

They gave us an extensive tour of three floors of fabrics and their design center. Then they served us strong coffee and let us interview a family member. After the store closed to customers, their co-owners helped Sweta choose the perfect sari, which Peter and I asked to pay for as a thank-you gift for Sweta, then they presented us with silk stoles.

All of my sari dreams were beyond fulfilled in India's oldest city. My sari cup runneth over.

# Master The Minutes

## *Day 80*
## *Pollachi, Tamil Nadu, India*

Lesson time. It's all coming together. I was waiting for another lesson, but one didn't come. I realize now that most lessons reveal themselves at the very end of our time in whichever region or country we are exploring. On the Camino, journaling was basically forced the last two weeks; with Rosemary, lessons came while we were driving away on a bus, but India had been quiet. There were struggles, then Divine gifts, but the lessons hadn't come together yet, until now.

Notes from our first weekend in Delhi support a personal experience Peter had earlier today. I find it ironic that it wasn't in the country's holiest cities, which we just visited — walking in the steps of Buddha and meditating on the Ganges in Varanasi where great saints (both past and present) congregate. Nope, it wasn't in any of those holy places where the lesson came. It was in the men's restroom at the Delhi airport.

Peter went to the bathroom to wash his hands after we indulged in some airport comfort food (vegetarian pizza and a vanilla latte) before heading to South India. When he walked in, he said he heard a melodic sound, but couldn't identify where it was coming from—a speaker, a bathroom stall, a cell phone?

When he turned to walk out, he saw a janitorial worker patiently waiting to get into an open stall to clean. The man was standing with his back to a wall, eyes closed, chanting softly. He was quietly singing to God.

For us, it was a perfect example of how to grow in our faith by making it a priority. This man had a quick break in his workday when he couldn't do anything else—and he chose to give that moment to God.

It reminded me of our time in Delhi where we took a Kriya yoga meditation class with Swami Smarananandaji. This was one of the classes that was similar to one I'd taken before and had no expectations of learning anything, but I was very wrong. Swamiji said, "goals are achieved in the minutes of our lives . . . and we are the masters of those minutes."

Peter's lesson: It doesn't matter if you're on the top floor with a corner office or if you're scrubbing a toilet—it's where your heart, thoughts, and consciousness are that matter.

# Sujatha

## Day 80
## Pollachi, Tamil Nadu, India

We are spending four days with a woman we consider our "Indian Auntie." We first met Sujatha a few years ago during a meditation retreat in India. During the retreat, a few hundred attendees boarded a private train together to make a day-long pilgrimage. Our train seats were next to Sujatha. During our travels, she shared with us about her meditation practice, her daughter who lives in Los Angeles, and what plants she uses for spices and medicine. She also told us we were welcome to come visit her anytime. So, we sent her a WhatsApp message and invited ourselves to her family's organic coconut farm in Pollachi, Tamil Nadu, which is in South India.

When we met her family, I immediately became fond of her mother-in-law. Her name is Shantha, which means peace. I liked calling her grandma—probably because I miss my own.

During our first meal together, Shantha suggested I get more servings of Sujatha's homemade caramel custard. She said, "the second serving will taste better. Third serving too." That's my kind of grandma.

# When You Need Them

## *Day 84*

## *Coimbatore, Tamil Nadu, India*

I had a lucid dream recently that came with a message, which Sujatha said almost word-for-word tonight.

In my dream, I was shot in the back by a person who was totally out of his mind. I stumbled to the street and waited for help, but help became harder and harder to get. Over and over I tried to convince people I was shot. I could see and feel the hole in my back, but they didn't help me.

Toward the end of my efforts, I saw a former friend from college sitting at a table at a bar. I saw him and knew he was my last chance to get help, but I was already disappointed because I knew his help would be difficult to get. I walked over to him anyway, and as if he was looking in my soul (like it was his body, but someone else was speaking through him), he said, "if you don't cultivate 'relationships,' they're not going to be there for you when you need them." I put part of that in quotes because it's a little fuzzy. Like I'm a news reporter in a courtroom waiting for a verdict to be announced and when the judge reads it, I'm so nervous that I temporarily become deaf. That actually happened once. I was working in Tulsa and still very new to reporting. Needless to say, I didn't have to report on court cases after that.

In my dream, as soon as he said, "they're not going to be there for you when you need them," I knew I was not going to get help. It felt like my dream body melted into the floor. I was without help. At that moment, the arms of my earth-body started to tingle, and I could feel my consciousness re-enter my body.

When I awoke, it was clear to me that the message was about my spiritual practices. If I don't pour into my meditation and mindfulness techniques, they're not going to be there for me when I need them.

To explain that further, the breathing and meditation techniques in the Kriya yoga practice help create a sense of calm, balance, gratitude and awareness. So, in times of stress or challenge, if I've done my spiritual practice homework by working on these techniques every day, then I should be able to tap into that sense of calm to help me navigate through the challenge.

I had blown off the dream, until the words came right back to me tonight in Coimbatore. Sujatha was telling us a story from Hindu mythology about a warrior implying he was a Brahmin. It was something like, if you misuse your weapons, "they won't be there for you when you need them."

What in the world is the exact message here?

I'm taking this as a lesson to all things necessary to me: relationships, meditation, my body and health. Take care of what you need, so it will "be there for you when you need them."

# Nice To Meet You, Shiva

## *Day 85*

## *Coimbatore, Tamil Nadu, India*

On an auspicious full-moon day, Sujatha took us to a historic Hindu temple in the western part of Coimbatore. It was built by King Karikala Chola in the 2nd Century, making it one of the oldest temples in the state of Tamil Nadu.

We made our way through it to pray before all of the deities (basically, statues that represent different aspects of God). We saved the biggest one for the end—Shiva, the first yogi.

As a welcome, a priest offered us some sandalwood powder to dip our finger in and place between our eyebrows (known as a tilaka). He said if we waited a while, we'd get to go closer to the puja. Puja means worship, and on this day, it was done by pouring cooked rice over the altar of Shiva. There were already a lot of people packed in line in front of us waiting to see the sacred offering.

We waited, waited some more, then some more. We were standing against a railing, which we used to keep ourselves steady while we attempted to do a standing meditation as we waited.

Sujatha (partially joking) said, "Kristin, you better ask Shiva to help us out." She had been teasing me that some small wishes I voiced were coming true that day.

I took the challenge and activated my full heart energy, which felt like a subtle vibration radiating from my chest outward.

Then I mentally chanted, "Shiva, I give you my soul, soul call . . . Shiva, I give you my soul, soul call."

The line of people started moving closer to the altar. No way! It's working? I tried to focus even harder. I took a step as the line moved forward and then kept inwardly chanting, "Shiva, I give you my soul, soul call."

Within a few minutes, we made it into the next room, which housed the altar near the far wall. The priest from earlier, made eye contact with me and motioned to come to him. Impossible, a dozen people were between us and they weren't moving, so there's no way I can just walk up to him. That doubt was proven wrong.

Sujatha guided us to the railing, which created a rectangular section in the middle of the room that only priests were allowed inside. The priest yelled, "come!" and motioned for me to open the gate and go into the priests' section. I fumbled with the gate and finally got it. Sujatha and Peter were right there with me as we moved inside the priests' section of the temple.

I kept inwardly chanting, "Shiva, I give you my soul, soul call," and envisioned a string in my heart being tugged toward the inner sanctuary of the temple, which was still 20 strides away. The path toward it, would also involve us walking past around 100 devout Hindus who were likely wondering why we were chosen to come forward. Sujatha later reminded me that we had waited a long time in line to earn our place, but the people watching us didn't know that.

We kept getting closer. One young priest wasn't happy about it and raised his arms as if saying, "What? Why are they in our section?" or "Why did you choose THEM, of all people?" But his resistance didn't seem to matter.

MY JOURNEY BACK TO GOD

The elder priest who had called for us, slowly ushered us all the way into the inner sanctuary of the temple. We made it. We were standing shoulder-to-shoulder in a small stone room. I was in the corner on the left and closest to the entry. I still couldn't see the actual idol that the priests were pouring the rice over, so I closed my eyes and continued chanting with my heart, "Shiva, I give you my soul, soul call."

The crowd of a dozen or so people was soon ushered out of the room.

We started to leave as well, walking clockwise in a circle like the people before us. We walked directly in front of the idol. It was beautiful and still a bit of a blur.

The idol is called a Shiva lingam (or Shiva linga). It gives form to the formless. To my eyes, it looked like a polished, black, stone cylinder. It sat on a circular base that looked like a flattened tea pot with a spout. Lingams can be all different sizes. This one was several feet tall and it was wrapped with garlands of flowers.

As I stood there in front of it, with my hands near my heart and in a prayer position, I was in awe. I said quickly, "thank you, Shiva."

Just then, a priest told me to move out of the way. As I stepped to the side, Sujatha and Peter passed me and exited the inner temple.

I started to leave. I turned one more time to thank Shiva for listening to my soul call and bringing us forward. As I did, two priests cut in front of me while carrying a giant steel pot of blessed offerings like fruit and flowers. They were heading out to hand them to the people waiting outside. The priests and their pot blocked my exit.

For a moment, I stood there in the most sacred space—alone. I just stared at the idol in shock.

Nice to meet you, Shiva.

I wondered, if you are this powerful, what else can you do? I don't necessarily want to witness it myself, but I believe it is possible.

Sujatha told us that day was especially sacred because it's a full moon and it's the only time that specific puja (the offering with cooked rice) was done on Shiva's altar.

Earlier that day, Sujatha took us to a newer Shiva temple at the Isha Yoga Center in Velliangiri. If the afternoon temple was one of the most ancient, this one was certainly the most modern. It felt like we were at a luxury wellness retreat.

The Isha Yoga Center has two energy pools where people can take a dip in the water to try and melt away their karmic blocks and raise their consciousness.

The pool for women is 30 feet below ground. After exchanging our clothes for a thick, orange dress, we showered and then descended down 32 steps to enter a clean, cold and golden pool.

Its water was charged with moon energy—at least that's what the "welcome" video said. I watched it after I thoroughly enjoyed floating in the pool while looking at a mural on the ceiling. It was just me and Sujatha in the women-only pool. The men's side was charged with sun energy and it had a lot more people.

While floating, I remembered I had met Shiva before.

Peter and I were spiritually married by a monk from Self-Realization Fellowship three months after our family wedding and five months after we signed our marriage certificate. The spiritual marriage happened during a weekend meditation retreat in Dallas. After the ceremony concluded with the monk showering us with blessed rose petals, we needed a witness to sign our vows, but we didn't know many people at the retreat. The first person we found was the Dallas-Fort Worth meditation groups' number one volunteer. His name is Shiva.

Shiva has been here the whole time, too.

I see Shiva like a powerful and loving grandfather. He's the God of arts and creativity, the first yogi, and the father of Ganesha.

Earlier, I remember hearing Swami Smarananandaji talk about experience. He said, "Experience is key to a devotee . . . experience God as love and joy."

The experiences that come to us in India are often challenging in some way. The outer challenges force the inner-self to evolve, learn, and absorb. On this day, we were able to experience God through Shiva—and each moment (at the historic temple and the modern one) was filled with love and joy.

If Jesus loved us through Rosemary, and Buddha loved us through Kiran, is Shiva working through Sujatha? Three months, three huge introductions.

All thanks to God's grace.

# Serve Your Role

## *Day 86*

## *Coimbatore, Tamil Nadu, India*

I'm sitting outside after meditation, breakfast, and seeing Sujatha leave for home. We board a train to Cochin later this afternoon at 1:30.

This morning, we woke up to the sound of chanting filling the retreat and meditation center. The building was originally a senior home. Small rooms line the outside of a grass and flower-filled courtyard.

Right now, two elder gardeners are trimming hedges using hand clippers and wearing plaid dhotis (a cotton fabric wrapped around their waists that looks like a combo of shorts and a skirt).

What a peaceful place this is. The elder woman in the kitchen just came out from working—likely preparing our coconut rice for lunch. She spoke loudly from the second-story over the courtyard to a young girl cleaning. They spoke in Tamil. Everyone smiled and they went back to work.

Last night, Sujatha was teasing me again about things I say coming to fruition. I silently thought of an impossible request for 8:15 at night, "chai!" I figured one last test after our day with Shiva couldn't hurt.

At around 9 p.m., the sweet elder in the kitchen randomly offered to make us chai and basically forced her friend

Sujatha to drink with us. My mind was once again blown by Shiva fulfilling even the tiniest request on our spirit-filled day.

Caffeine, a tablespoon of sugar, and the end of a few magical days together likely inspired our late-night conversation that was filled with laughter. As we chatted, Sujatha was sharing about her inner mantra that keeps her above any unnecessary mental drama. "Serve your role, and don't think about its fruits." Basically, do your duty in this life and don't concern yourself with its rewards, recognition, or useless drama.

# The Beginning Of Something Beautiful

## Day 96

### Noida, Uttar Pradesh, India

*"Jesus replied, 'You do not realize now what I am doing, but later you will understand.'" John 13:7, NIV*

Toward the end of our longest meditation yet as a couple— six hours— Peter and I, along with 100 or so other people, chanted, "jai, jai, Ram" in the basement temple of an ashram outside of New Delhi.

"Jai, jai, Ram" has roots in Sanskrit and means "victory to God."

A young monk led us through the second half of the meditation, which included this extended chanting session. His voice had a sweet depth that was both soul-stirring and a delight to my ears. My heart felt full.

As we chanted, I realized this was the end of our three-month pilgrimage. I felt tightness in my throat. It's where emotion seems to get stuck in my body, but this time, it was a good emotion. In the past, it's where anxiety or anger would reside. During a counseling session, I learned that when the tightness comes to my throat, I need to place my hands on my neck and tell my throat, "you're safe, you have nothing to be afraid of."

I continued chanting, "jai, jai, Ram, jai, jai, Ram" feeling the peaceful vibration from the chant resonate in my throat. My vocal cords started to relax. "Jai, jai, Ram, jai, jai, Ram." I wanted to use that new vibration of peace, love and gratitude at a time when I needed it earlier in my life—during my breaking points. They were the moments when I didn't have the strength to speak up for myself.

I mentally went back to my former-boss's office. It was the day that ended with me questioning my worth. I saw myself sitting there in his small, glassed-in office, throat tight, unable to speak. He said a lot of things that day, and what I heard was, "You'll never be good enough."

As I sat across from him in his office, the tears started to well-up in my eyes, then fall. The first, then the second. As they fell, I knew I was showing even more weakness by crying—proof that I never would be good enough.

As the meditation neared its final hour, I thought I'd use the positive chanting vibration to mentally recreate the scenario in my boss's office. Maybe I'd confidently tell him something . . . anything. But that's not what happened. Instead, I had a vision.

I saw something in my mind's eye, and it wasn't coming from my own creativity. It was like watching a play and not having any idea what was going to happen next.

In the vision, I saw myself sitting in my boss's office crying. Then, a second version of me appeared—she was sitting in the chair next to the me that was crying. She leaned over to me and quietly whispered in my ear, "this is the beginning of something beautiful."

My boss was still talking down to me. I was still crying. But the second me continued whispering and the side of her mouth now cracked with a smile. She continued, "I know this is hard right now, and it's going to be difficult for a while, but something great is going to come from this very moment."

In the meditation room, the tears started flowing. I remembered that the blue bandana I wore on the Camino was in my chair and I grabbed it to start wiping my face.

"Jai, jai, Ram, jai, jai, Ram, jai, jai, Ram."

I thought about how much had happened since that challenging moment in my boss's office. We had completed a life-changing faith walk that took me and Peter across three countries—drawing us closer to God and each other. Over and over, I thought of her words, "this is the beginning of something beautiful." She was right, and it all started with that one moment.

As the chanting continued, my tears of gratitude continued to flow so hard I stopped wiping them away.

"Jai, jai, Ram, jai, jai, Ram."

# Final Gifts Of Our Pilgrimage

## Day 96

## Indira Gandhi International Airport, New Delhi, Delhi, India

I'm at the Delhi airport about to go through security. In India, women and men are separated before going through security so women can be screened by a woman behind a curtain with a wand.

I look ahead to my queue options and there are three lines I can choose from. I chose one. It ends up being the longest and slowest line. The female security guard is a square-set woman and she looks tough. I ponder switching lines but decide to ride it out. All of our camera gear is in our carry-on luggage, so Peter and I are both a bit wary about a security guard confiscating all of the footage we've captured the last three months; however, we have been pretty fortunate through security so far.

A week or so earlier, one female security guard was also very intimidating, but when she saw my dimples she lit up. While wanding me and checking my pockets, she told me that her son has dimples, too. He's eight months old.

The curtain in front of me opens and the square-set officer waives me to come forward into her small fabric stall. I stand on the platform in silence, raise my arms and await the patting and wanding.

I hear her humming. How impressive that she is effectively doing a very repetitive and tedious job on the outside, while on the inside, she's in her happy place. Her humming gets louder. Then she starts to sing. "It goes like this the fourth, the fifth." This time, I lit up. "I know that song!" "the nah nah nah the major lift!" was my attempt to remember the words on cue. Oh, the unexpected joy! We exchanged huge smiles as my wanding was completed. I left with her inner bliss now in my head. "Hallelujah . . . Hallelu—u—jah."

I've been asking myself lately if I've changed. One way is that I feel more neutral.

While floating with Shiva, I realized that's how I want to live life. I want to float through it, never sinking too low in the valleys or rising too high during the peaks of what life brings—just somewhere in the middle. Neutral buoyancy.

So far, this neutral feeling has affected my decision making. While we were staying with Rosemary, I noticed it was harder for me to make a few simple decisions—not because they became more difficult, but because I cared less. I know that inwardly I'd feel the same no matter what the outcome of the decision.

I first noticed it when she asked if we wanted to pay money to see the inside of Roman ruins south of Haifa. I literally could not decide. It didn't matter because either way I was just so relaxed. I knew I'd be feeling that same relaxation if we walked around the ruins or if we just admired them from outside the security gate. We ended up skipping the first round of ruins then paying to see the second, which included a theater. I used Google Maps to preview the visuals before purchasing the ticket, which helped.

I'm wondering how long this will last—the peace that was built up during these last three months? I hope it lasts. I also hope Peter and I are able to spread this peace to those around us as we reintegrate to living with our families. I've also noticed that I'm eating less. This will be the real challenge as we get back to our mothers' cooking. I know my body will feel better if I don't overeat, even if it's really tasty.

I had a bit of a head cold for one day after flying back to Delhi from Coimbatore. It was easier for me to hear my body tell me what it wanted and didn't want. Feeling a bit ill, it definitely did not want sugar. Not even chai with sugar. It didn't want a lot of food, just enough. My mind would say, "no way," and my actions would listen.

# Home

# One Week Later

## *Vero Beach, Florida, USA*

After returning home from this pilgrimage, my mom took me to a Brooks and Dunn concert. As a kid, I sang the words to their song, "Brand New Man" countless times. This time as I sang, one lyric had new meaning, "Oh, how I used to roam, I was a Rolling Stone." That one lyric, perfectly combined the repetitive message to "roam" that started this entire adventure, and the Bob Dylan song that kept coming to me while walking across Spain, "How does it feel? To be without a home, like a complete unknown, like a rolling stone."

On the flight to meet my mom, I sat next to a pastor who shared one of his sermons that included an analogy of *Wizard of Oz*. When he mentioned the "yellow brick road," I realized I had heard those three words together at least three times over the past few days.

A quick Google search popped up a lesson from the *Wizard of Oz*. Dorothy and her friends follow the yellow brick road, only to realize they had what they were looking for the whole time.

For me, that's God. He's within us, around us. This pilgrimage has brought me closer to Him and in more forms than I ever would have imagined: Jesus, Buddha, Shiva, and countless friends and strangers who took care of us, taught us and guided us.

To those of them, and to all of you, thank you for going on this journey with us.

# One Year Later

## *Dallas, Texas, USA*

It's been one year to the day since Peter and I left for our pilgrimage. It was a big "leave" because we left everything that we had prioritized for a long time: our jobs, a physical home, belongings, a lifestyle of structure and consistency.

We left that former world for a life of wandering, homelessness (by choice), and minimalism.

I need to point out the stark contrast of our lives from that moment we left for our pilgrimage.

On this day, one year after leaving everything material that we held dear, we experienced a day of the finest worldly offerings.

We started the day taking photos at one of the fanciest and exclusive hotels in Dallas, Texas, followed by massages and Peter's first hydro-facial, a breakfast of avocado toast, Greek yogurt, fruit, granola and a whole carafe of coffee. Afterward, we took a brief swim in the hotel's roof-top pool, then went to dinner at Nobu—where I ate the most delicious Japanese meal, which included seven courses of sushi, lobster, imported Wagyu steak, two desserts and a cappuccino. Did I mention we didn't have to pay for any of this?

We are here on assignment, documenting our weekend staycation for a new, local, NBC television show called *Texas Today*. The show was created when we were halfway through our pilgrimage, which was the text I received in Israel. We didn't have any idea this opportunity would be finalized and then offered to us three months after we returned back to the US.

We left knowing we had to—because God opened so many doors for us that He proved we were working in the right direction. But before those doors could open, others had to slam shut—and they did. It hurt, but it was, "the beginning of something beautiful."

I'll admit, the decision to accept this job, which would have me returning to the television station that was so hard for me to leave, was one of the most difficult decisions of my life. This is how I made the decision: when two thoughts entered my mind, I'd get goosebumps on my arms. Those thoughts are, "you'll need the people in the building," and "unexpected opportunities."

My new job has offered plenty of unexpected opportunities. It consistently and gently pushes me out of my comfort zone—to have fun, to be brave, to speak up, to not be pushed around, and to enjoy the earthy offerings of this human experience. Today, though, has been the most extreme of the earthly offerings.

We estimated that our six ounces of Wagyu cost $220. That's just for the meat, not for the expertise of the brilliant person who perfectly prepared it and then lit it on fire at our table while dousing it with Cognac.

The steak melted in my mouth. I barely had to chew.

Do you think this extreme day of earthly gifts—happening on the one-year anniversary of leaving everything worldly behind us—is a coincidence?

Or is it a Divine gift for taking a risk to follow what we heard as a calling to reconnect with God, our faith, and each other?

The thought that immediately comes to my mind when I ask myself these questions is also the name of a book, *Jump, and the Net Will Appear.*

KRISTIN DICKERSON

.